The Beatles... The Easy Way: A Guide To The Official Recordings

Andrew Greenaway

Dedicated to Lilian and Steve Greenaway –
my mother and brother –
without whom I may never have dug the Beatles

The Beatles... The Easy Way: A Guide To The Official Recordings

Andrew Greenaway

WP
WYMER
PUBLISHING
Bedford, England

First published in Great Britain in 2014
by Wymer Publishing
www.wymerpublishing.co.uk
Wymer Publishing is a trading name of Wymer (UK) Ltd

ISBN 978-1-908724-08-3

Edited by Jeremy Francis-Broom.

Typeset by Wymer (UK) Ltd
Printed and bound by Lightning Source

A catalogue record for this book is available from the British Library.

Cover design by Andy Francis.

Contents

Introduction

The purpose of this book is to guide you through the artist's career step by step as it happened. Listed chronologically are all the major releases, promotional records and media recordings that make up the full body of recordings produced by the artist and in most cases, officially released, although some recordings may remain in part or full, unreleased.

It is not an "anorak's paradise" and doesn't list numerous variants of each release. In fact it centres on the UK and USA releases, which are arguably the major markets. That said, it is also worth pointing out that invariably most European countries releases mirrored those of the UK, and likewise Canadian releases did so with USA. Some non UK / USA releases are listed, where they are of particular interest, most notably if they contain material that was not available on UK or USA releases at the time, even though it may have appeared in these territories in subsequent years, either in part or full.

With each entry the original format of its release is indicated in brackets with the following abbreviations:
SP = single play vinyl
EP = extended play vinyl
LP = long play album vinyl
CP = live performance
MC = Cassette
VHS = video home system, analogue videotape.
CD = compact disc album
CDs = compact disc single
DVD = digital versatile disc
DD = digital download

The objective of this tome is to comprehensively guide you through the recordings with detailed information about them, and to help those who are not fully au fait with all of the artist's work to have a better understanding of what happened and when. And in the case of changing line-ups; as to who played on what is fully documented, as sometimes even the record companies provided incorrect credits on the releases!

Preface

Just what the world needs, eh? Another book on The Beatles. But when Wymer asked if I'd write one, I jumped at the chance. I've always loved music, but the Beatles' music was the first to really hook me, reel me in, gut me and devour me - whole.

They mean so much to me. I grew up listening to them. When I sing along to their early songs, I start to fill up. When I hear their later songs, they blow my mind.

How many people do you think have written books about the Beatles? Hundreds, yeah? And how many people have shaken hands with Paul McCartney – since he was knighted for services to music, and on Ringo's birthday? Not many, correct? And how many have done both and are still alive today? Well, there's me!

For the record, I went to see Steely Dan at the Hammersmith Apollo on their Heavy Rollers tour on 7 July 2007. My friend worked for a ticket company that knew which VIP guests would be in attendance and where. As the band launched into its encore of 'Kid Charlemagne', I suddenly needed to visit the loo. I ensured my route back passed by Sir Paul. I stopped before him and gave him the old thumbs aloft. He shook my hand with a big grin. It was a nice moment. Yes of course I washed my hands after I'd finished peeing. I haven't since, mind.

And that's my qualification for penning this! And anyway, there's always room for another book on something so phenomenal, right? No, Scroobius Pip: they weren't just a band. They may have a few detractors today who can't understand why they are so highly praised by the many, so hopefully this book will shed light on why anyone who bad-mouths McCartney for singing at the Queen's Diamond Jubilee Concert should just STFU and listen to 'For No One'.

I clearly remember queuing up with my mum and brother to see *A Hard Day's Night* at the Commodore cinema in Orpington High Street. I would have been six years old. I don't think I was wearing my shiny black plastic Beatles wig at the time, but I could be wrong. I know we bought some *Findus* fish fingers on the way home, which came with free black and white photographs of the lads: if memory serves, brother Steve snatched Paul so I got lumbered with John.

Although having an older brother to share in the phenomenon that was Beatlemania invariably meant I ended up with the 'I Love Ringo' pin badge, it didn't bother me. I loved them all equally, and seeing Ringo talk about his last meeting with George in Martin Scorsese's *All Things Must Pass* documentary affected me every bit as much as hearing Paul sing 'Here Today' for John. Probably more, in fact. I mean, come on – that scene would melt the coldest heart. But I digress. And you'll find I do that a fair bit. Occasionally for good reason. And there are many personal recollections and esoteric references included too. I trust none of these will be too distracting for you, lovely reader. They may even make you chuckle.

As you're reading this (and thank you so much for picking it up, and maybe even coughing up some hard-earned dosh), I imagine you have some knowledge of the band. Hence certain assumptions have been made. You know the individual band members' names, that they all hailed from Liverpool, conquered the world, took drugs, invented biscuits, grew beards and broke up squabbling over money. As the publisher's introduction infers, it's not necessarily a book for the die-hard fan but more for the new or casual follower. But of course I hope some devotees read it and resist any temptation to ridicule me; in the parlance of our times, DPMO. I'm just cheese. But if I should remind them of at least one long-forgotten Fab fact, I'll be a happy man.

Perhaps to explain a little further why this is not the anoraks guide that it could be, I have focussed on UK releases (including compilations) because that's where the band hailed from, and because the US releases initially (both singles and albums – oh, and extended players) were effectively compilations, with three to four fewer tracks on the albums than their nearest UK counterpart – as George was to complain, "When the American company released albums like *Yesterday... And Today*, we didn't have anything to do with them. They always put out more albums in the States. If we put out two singles and two albums [in the UK], they'd convert them into three albums by keeping the extra tracks." So if I have 'reviewed' something once, I'm not gonna blather about it some more just for the sake of weighing your book shelf down (or to eating up your Kindle's memory). No piggin' way.

Also, I've not dwelt too much on the differences between the mono and stereo versions of their records. That could probably fill another book – in fact it does: *The Beatles In Mono* by another Andrew (kudos, Mr Hickey!) – but not this one.

Nor does this book provide you with a painstaking analysis/deconstruction of each of their songs: *Revolution In The Head* by the late Ian MacDonald has already done that quite magnificently.

And for a comprehensive history of the band, there's nothing to touch Mark Lewisohn's *All These Years* trilogy.

No, my aim is to hopefully help newbies get better acquainted with the fabulous music within the 'core catalogue', in much the same way that 2000's seemingly pointless 1 album reached a whole new generation of fans. And if it succeeds in getting you to seek out the books mentioned above, then job done.

The June 2012 closure of the Beatlemania museum in Hamburg due to a lack of interest after just three years is another reason to big-up the mop-tops. But at least Ringo's birthplace has been saved from demolition!

It's easy for anyone born after 1970 to underestimate the cultural significance of the Beatles and dismiss their importance. even to this day when someone breaks big, who do they get compared to? Sure, many of the records the band set may have since been broken, but will people still be quoting lines from *Spice World: The Movie* fifty years after its release? Did Take That and Westlife have the same level of success on both sides of the Atlantic? And, unlike the Justin Bieber albums, it didn't take an army of writers and producers to create what they did.

It's hard to think of anyone who's had success since the Beatles whose music wasn't influenced in one way or another by the band – either their compositional skills, the technological advances they oversaw and actively encouraged in the studio, their live performances (their 1965 concert at Shea Stadium heralded what we all know today as arena rock) or the official recordings that are, without question, a national treasure-trove.

Hopefully this book will provide ample evidence of the natural talent and innovation of four young lads who unintentionally shook the world in a way that no one is likely to do ever again – certainly not in my lifetime, anyhow.

Thank you. You've got a lucky face.

Andrew Greenaway
Somewhere in England
30 January 2014

MY BONNIE / THE SAINTS (WHEN THE SAINTS GO MARCHING IN)

German Release: Polydor SPLHM237112, October 1961 (SP)
UK Release: Polydor LPHM46612, 5 January 1962 (SP)
US Release: MGM K-13213, 27 January 1964 (SP)
Recording data: 22 June 1961, Friedrich-Ebert-Halle and Studio Rahlstedt, Hamburg-Harburg, Germany
Producer: Bert Kaempfert
Engineer: Karl Hinze

In August 1960, the sort-of-managed by Allan Williams Beatles – consisting of John Lennon (vocals/guitar), Paul McCartney (vocals/guitar), George Harrison (lead guitar/vocals), Stu Sutcliffe (bass/occasional vocals) and new recruit Pete Best (drums) - started the first of five lengthy stints in Hamburg, with a residency at the Indra Club. It is generally agreed that for the next two years, Hamburg is where the group learned its craft and transformed from a fairly ordinary skiffle group into the band that would ultimately conquer the world. They certainly became a formidable unit, both musically and vocally, and Lennon and McCartney would begin to gain confidence in their songwriting abilities while in Germany. To be sure, their time in the Fatherland gave rise to Lennon's later "I might have been born in Liverpool - but I grew up in Hamburg" quote, which acknowledges the songwriting duo's heathen chemistry.

The band moved from the Indra up to the Kaiserkeller, and then on to the Top Ten Club, before the underage Harrison (just 17) was kicked out of the country in violation of German child protection laws. Shortly thereafter, McCartney and Best were deported for setting fire to a "rubber johnny", so Lennon and (eventually) Sutcliffe also returned to Liverpool - and the Cavern Club.

A second stay in Hamburg lasted from April until July 1961, and it was while at the Top Ten again that the Beatles made their first professional recordings. Sutcliffe had just decided to leave the band to pursue a career in art in Germany (where he would die as the result of brain aneurysm in April 1962), so McCartney reluctantly took over on bass. The band was paid about £25 each, with no royalty rights, for a recording session as back-up band for English rock and roll singer/songwriter/guitarist Tony Sheridan. They were also to record two songs without Sheridan: the roaring 20s hit 'Ain't She Sweet', and the Lennon/Harrison composed instrumental 'Beatle Bop' which, unbeknownst to the band, was renamed 'Cry For A Shadow' due to its similarity to the sounds of Cliff Richard's backing band and which (along with other 'Beat Brothers' Hamburg recordings) would be cunningly issued in a variety of different formats by *Polydor* once the Beatles became famous. But 'My Bonnie' and 'The Saints' were the first to be released, credited to Tony Sheridan and The Beat Brothers (as that name was reputedly more understandable for the German audience than The Beatles: "We went along with it – it was a record!" McCartney commented later). Lennon deemed the record "terrible. It could have been anybody."

The sessions were instigated/overseen by Bert Kaempfert, a well-known Hamburger, musician and composer, in charge of production for *Polydor Records*. Kaempfert is best remembered for his big instrumental hit 'Wonderland By Night' (Wunderland bei Nacht), which reached number one this very same year. He also composed the music for the 1966 Frank Sinatra hit, 'Strangers In the Night'. During the Beatles sessions, he had Best's bass drum removed because the hapless drummer kept playing too fast.

Not being a song penned or sung by the band, and not even being truly representative of the Beatles' Hamburg sound, 'My Bonnie' is nevertheless regarded as the first Beatles single – and without it, things may have been very different.

To get an idea of the band's time in Hamburg - and the relationship between Lennon and Sutcliffe - you could do much worse than watch Iain Softley's film *Backbeat*. And also get hold of a copy of Allan Williams' memoir, *The Man Who Gave The Beatles Away*. (During the 70s, Williams played a key role in various Beatles conventions - indeed, this author met him at Europe's first Christmas Beatle Convention at London's Alexandra Palace in December 1976). Oh, and it goes without saying that Mark Lewisohn's meticulously researched *Tune In* covers this period comprehensively.

Now read on...

LOVE ME DO / P.S. I LOVE YOU

UK Release: Parlophone R 4949, 5 October 1962 (SP)
US Release: Tollie T-9008, 27 April 1964 (SP)
Recording data: 4 and 11 September 1962, EMI Studios, London
Producer: George Martin
Engineer: Norman Smith

"It was quite hard to come in singing 'Love Me Do'. We thought our numbers were a bit wet. But we gradually broke that down and decided to try them." **– John Lennon**

The band's first single proper. And so the story goes, Raymond Jones ordered a copy of 'My Bonnie' in NEMS (the North End Music Store) in the heart of Liverpool. The store was run by one Brian Epstein, and this request ultimately led him to manage the Beatles (despite Williams telling him not to touch them with "a fucking bargepole"), touting their music hither and thither. *EMI* was Epstein's first choice, but they were unimpressed by the unrepresentative Hamburg recordings, and declined to sign the band in December 1961. The Beatles were then famously rejected by *Decca* following a disastrous audition on New Year's Day. On realising the error of their ways, *Decca* subsequently snapped up the Rolling Stones. But that was after a chance meeting with Syd Coleman, of *EMI*-owned publishers Ardmore & Beechwood, that led Eppy to George Martin and in through the out door back to *EMI*. Way to go, Mr Jones!

Actually, in his book *With The Beatles*, Epstein's personal assistant at that time, Alistair Taylor, claims he invented the name 'Raymond Jones' just to ensure Epstein ordered the single because he was fed-up with so many people asking after it. Taylor later became general manager for NEMS and, briefly, *Apple Corps*, and was christened 'Mr Fixit' by the band. He was there, so who are we to argue? Well I'm going to anyway: I don't believe Mr Epstein would tell fibs and therefore Mr Jones was real. And furthermore, his parents were Desmond and Molly. So there.

For *EMI* to release a debut single of two original compositions was pretty bold in 1962 – although I didn't know this at the time. I was four years old. And here's the thing: many people who wax lyrical about the impact the band had, never seem to take into account the millions who were just caught up in the excitement at the time. It was just a happy coincidence that they truly did turn out to be something special that in later life we wouldn't be a dot embarrassed about.

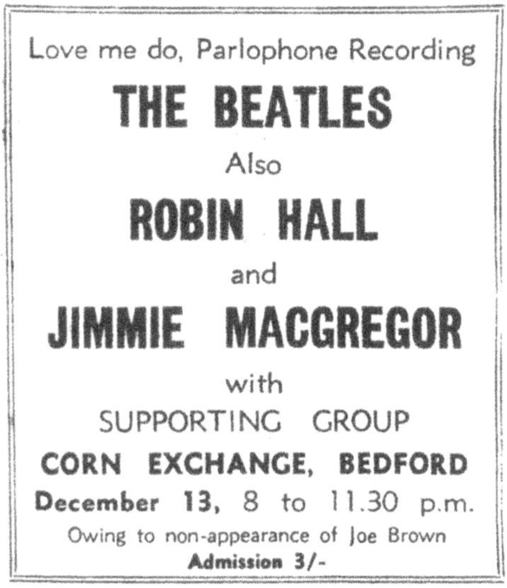

Both sides of this debut platter were largely penned by McCartney, and embellished by Lennon, heralding the start of one of the greatest song writing partnerships of the 20th century. Don't argue... although, as we will find, there were to be very many 'solo' efforts along the way. But when the pair forged the masterplan that would hold good throughout the life of the band, they agreed to credit one another and split the royalties. Now that's teamwork.

The band recorded three different

versions of 'Love Me Do' at Abbey Road in 1962, all featuring different drummers. When they first auditioned for *EMI* - and producer George Martin – on 6 June 1962, their drummer was Pete Best (who had played on 'My Bonnie'). In the intervening period, before cutting this single, Best had been ousted. This decision (actioned by Epstein) had the support of the other three Beatles, but wasn't an easy move – not least because their faithful friend and roadie Neil Aspinall – affectionately referred to as 'Nel' by the boys – was in a illicit relationship with Best's mother, Mona, and indeed sired Pete's half-brother Vincent "Roag" (born 21 July 1962).

Best's replacement was Ringo Starr, who had first met The Beatles when they were playing in Hamburg where he was drumming with another Liverpool band, Rory Storm And The Hurricanes. He would occasionally sit in with Lennon, McCartney and Harrison, and he was their first choice to replace Best.

Although Starr played drums on the 'Love Me Do' single, Martin had the band re-record it later in September for their first long player with session drummer Andy White - though Starr did at least play tambourine on that version. The Best version (but not the best version) eventually surfaced on Anthology 1 in 1995.

Oh, and here's yet another thing: despite his much shorter tenure with the band, Best put in far more hours behind the drum kit on stage with the Beatles than Starr. It seems that being the really quiet one was his downfall. Like me, he went on to become a Civil Servant. But not before being asked to take over the drum seat behind Rory Storm – as Starr's replacement – and then the Epstein managed Merseybeats (Epstein wanted to mould the band into another Beatles). He declined both offers.

Martin was to play a key role in the development of the Beatles and, like quite a few others, is often referred to as "the fifth Beatle" (a title that he probably deserves more than t'others, truth be told, even if he himself doesn't care that much for it; but in musical terms, he clearly trumps their loyal pal, Neil Aspinall). Martin had previously worked for the *BBC's* classical music department, and joined *EMI* in 1950. For much of that decade, he produced comedy and novelty records, working with the likes of Peter Sellers and Spike Milligan (both of whom first came to prominence in the British radio comedy programme, *The Goon Show*). In 1955, Martin took on responsibility for *EMI's* subsidiary label, *Parlophone Records*, which was used for their less significant acts. Keen to add rock and roll to the label's repertoire, Martin found the perfect hit-makers in the Beatles, who helped transform *Parlophone* and, ultimately, the *EMI Group* itself. His association with Sellers and Milligan greatly impressed the Beatles, whose humour was hugely influenced by *The Goon Show*.

The lyrics to B-side 'P.S. I Love You' are written like a letter – a ploy McCartney would utilise later with songs such as 'Paperback Writer' and 'When I'm Sixty-Four'. This song was recorded at the same session as the album version of 'Love Me Do' and thus also features White on drums, with Starr on maracas. Kind of ironically, Swedish actress Britt Ekland used 'P.S. I Love You' to woo Peter Sellers, who she married in 1964.

In the mid-70s, after all that the band had achieved, Starr said of 'Love Me Do', "For me, that was more important than anything else. That first piece of plastic. You can't believe how great that was. It was so wonderful. We were on a record!" Thirty-six years after The Beatles' version, Starr recorded a cover of 'Love Me Do', with Aerosmith's Steven Tyler on harmonica, for his *Vertical Man* solo album.

The song's simple plea for love essentially became the group's manifesto, with McCartney some years later citing it as the Beatles' "greatest philosophical song".

At the time, though, producer Martin thought the lyrics a tad trite. And when Tony Sheridan first heard the record, he was amazed how the band had suddenly gone from being one of the best rhythm and blues groups around to "pleasing the teenies".

Released the same day as the first ever James Bond movie, *Dr No*, and a week and a bit before the Cuban missile crisis when many people thought the end of the world was nigh.

PLEASE PLEASE ME / ASK ME WHY

UK Release: Parlophone R 4983, 11 January 1963 (SP)
US Release: Vee-Jay VJ 498, 7 February 1963 (SP)
Recording data: 26 November 1962, EMI Studios, London
Producer: George Martin
Engineer: Norman Smith

"We tried to make it as simple as possible. Some of the stuff we've written in the past has been a bit way-out, but we aimed this one straight at the hit parade." – **John Lennon**

With nuclear holocaust averted, Martin wanted the band to release their recording of Mitch Murray's 'How Do You Do It?' as their follow-up to 'Love Me Do'. But the band insisted on issuing one of their own songs, and this was when – in McCartney's words – Martin "showed that he could see beyond what we were offering him... George said, 'Well, we'll put the tempo up,' He lifted the tempo and we all thought that was much better." On completion of taping 'Please Please Me', the won-over producer proudly announced that the boys had just recorded their first number one. He was kind of right, as it eventually made it to the top of the charts published by *Melody Maker*, *New Musical Express* and *Disc*. However, in lieu of a standard singles chart at that time, the *Record Retailer* chart was later deemed the official one, and 'Please Please Me' only made it to number two there.

Whatever, The Beatles' first national UK television appearance, on *Thank Your Lucky Stars* on 19 January 1963, no doubt assisted this single to almost reach the toppermost of the poppermost.

By now, the band's look, under Epstein's guidance, had changed dramatically from the scruffy leather trousers, jackets and boots they wore in Hamburg to smart suits, made by Soho tailor Dougie Millings. At the time, I lived right next door to Dougie's brother, Geoff, who would taunt me and my brother with snaps of his sibling with the boys. We were well jel.

Like 'Love Me Do', Lennon's harmonica playing features prominently on a song that came to him while listening to Roy Orbison's 'Only The Lonely'. Lyrically, the quaint old Bing Crosby song 'Please' was influential - and the song was most certainly not a plea for reciprocal oral pleasurings. Oh no! The vocal stylings of the Everly Brothers on 'Cathy's Clown' inspired Lennon and McCartney's performance, which they worked on after Martin urged them to 'pep' the arrangement up a gnat's.

'Ask Me Why' was another of the band's original compositions – primarily

BEDFORD RECORD FEBRUARY 12 1963

BEDFORD'S TOP TEN

1	Diamonds	JET HARRIS AND TONY MEEHAN	Decca
2	Up on the Roof	KENNY LYNCH	HMV
3	Telstar	THE TORNADOES	Decca
4	Globetrotter	THE TORNADOES	Decca
5	Queen For Tonight	HELEN SHAPIRO	Columbia
6	Love Me Do	THE BEATLES	Parlophone
7	Dance On	THE SHADOWS	Columbia
8	Return to Sender	ELVIS PRESLEY	RCA
9	All Alone Am I	BRENDA LEE	Brunswick
10	Bossa Nova USA	DAVE BRUBECK	CBS

The Beatles are only one group among so many, and are touring in "one - nighters" purely on the strength of one hit record, "Love Me Do", which they composed and wrote themselves. It's a fine song, well delivered, but they had better get their pens out once again and find another hit to qualify a continued success We don't think "Please Please Me" will provide the answer.

penned by Lennon – that they were regularly performing live and were confident about including in their audition for *EMI* on 6 June. Another Lennon/McCartney song, 'Tip Of My Tongue', was considered for the b-side of 'Please Please Me', but was eventually ditched in favour of this Smokey Robinson And The Miracles flavoured tune. The band never officially released 'Tip Of My Tongue', which was bequeathed to fellow Liverpudlain Tommy Quickly, who promptly failed to score with it.

The Beatles half-hearted rendition of 'How Do You Do It?' was eventually released on *Anthology 1*. Gerry & the Pacemakers, another Scouse band managed by Epstein and recorded by Martin, made a far better fist of it, releasing it as their debut single a few months after 'Please Please Me'. It went straight to number one, but an unrepentant Lennon would say, "Lot's of shit rises to the top of the charts. We don't do shit." Gerry was knocked off the top by the Beatles' next single. But there was to be a long player first...

© Sipa Press / Rex

PLEASE PLEASE ME

UK Release: Parlophone PMC 1202 (mono) / PCS 3042 (stereo), 26 March 1963 (LP)
Recording data: 4 and 11 September, 26 and 30 November 1962; 11, 20 and 25 February 1963, EMI Studios, London
Producer: George Martin
Engineer: Norman Smith
Tracks: I Saw Her Standing There / Misery / Anna (Go To Him) / Chains / Boys / Ask Me Why / Please Please Me / Love Me Do / P.S. I Love You / Baby It's You / Do You Want To Know A Secret / A Taste Of Honey / There's A Place / Twist And Shout.

"I'd been up to the Cavern and I'd seen what they could do and I said, Let's record every song you've got. Come down to the studios, and we just whistled through them in a day."
– George Martin

"We found the whole thing quite funny - we had to come in the back entrance, because we were not allowed in the control room. So we were like a gang of cheeky schoolboys sneaking in there, looking up at the glass and giggling a bit. To be given a chance was exciting, but we were quite amused by it at the same time." ***– Paul McCartney***

And so, the debut album: Rush-released to capitalise on the success of the first two singles, *Please Please Me* comprised the songs the band were playing live at the time. With over half of them penned by McCartney and Lennon, this added to what made them stand out at the time: a proper band playing their own instruments and writing their own songs. Early on, it was clear that they were a bit special. And they even made 'Twist And Shout' their own.

Originally performed by The Top Notes as 'Shake It Up, Baby' - produced by Phil Spector - the Beatles' version was actually much closer to the Isley Brothers' subsequent cover. The Isley's rendition was produced by Bert Russell, who co-wrote the song with Phil Medley. Russell wanted to show Spector how the song was supposed to sound, and at the same time helped the Brothers achieve their first top twenty hit. The Beatles replicated both the arrangement and energy of this version, but Lennon's phlegm-fuelled vocal took it to another level.

Lennon had a heavy cold during their marathon first full album session on 11 February 1963, when the band recorded 11 songs in just 10 hours. Martin saved 'Twist And Shout' till last as he knew Lennon wouldn't be able to sing anything else after (indeed, a second take had to be abandoned). And you can hear the affect of the cold and the strain on his vocal chords. Brilliant! What a way to end a record.

And what a way to start one, too (...three, four)! 'I Saw Her Standing There' was originally titled simply 'Seventeen', and sounds nothing like the Sex Pistols' song of the same name from their own debut album, which was originally titled 'I'm Lazy Sod'. Why am I mentioning the Sex Pistols? Well, like it or not, they too had a huge impact on popular music, and also changed a member of their rhythm section just before recording their first album. And they played their last concert in San Francisco in the merry month of August. Just saying.

'I Saw Her Standing There' was a lively number the band had been using to open their shows. The lyrics were inspired by a young judy called Iris Caldwell, the brother of Rory Storm, whom McCartney dated for a couple of years. Harrison also considered her to be his first coo ca choo (when she was just twelve), but she went on to marry Alvin Stardust.

The song used the bass line from Chuck Berry's 'I'm Talking About You', a ditty the band played in Hamburg, and was the first Beatles' song to feature the high falsetto "Whooh!" that was to become a trademark of their early hits.

Lennon and McCartney wrote 'Misery' in early 1963 for singer Helen Shapiro, then just 16 years old, who they were supporting on their first ever national tour of Britain. The song was rejected though by Shapiro's producer. She was unaware of this, and later complained, "I never got to hear it or give an opinion. It's a shame, really." But the song did still achieve the distinction of being the first Beatles' song to be covered by another artist: Kenny Lynch, who was on that same tour with Shapiro, and who much later appeared on the cover of McCartney's *Band On The Run* album. Lynch had a smash/flop single with his pop-orientated interpretation of 'Misery' a few months later.

'Anna (Go To Him)' was originally a minor hit for American country soul singer Arthur Alexander in September 1962, and was a particular favourite of Lennon's. Bereft of its string backing, The Beatles' version is generally regarded as superior, with the boys' backing vocals also being more effective.

Although most of the album's lead vocals are by Lennon and/or McCartney, Starr gets to sing 'Boys' (which was also his solo spot with Rory Storm And The Hurricanes), while Harrsion got Goffin and King's 'Chains' and had a song specially composed for him by Lennon and McCartney. 'Do You Want To Know A Secret' was heavily influenced by 'I'm Wishing' from *Snow White And The Seven Dwarfs*, which Lennon's mum used to sing to him as a nipper.

Like 'Boys', 'Baby It's You' was first a hit for African-American girl group The Shirelles, and shows that the band weren't afraid to be associated with lyrics written for women – their 'a good song is a good song' approach was another reason for their imminent mass appeal. That, and the fact that they were able to match (and often beat) the quality of the songs they had initially covered. Word for word, note for note.

An instrumental version of 'A Taste Of Honey' had recently been a hit single for English clarinettist Acker Bilk, who (with his Paramount Jazz Band) had dominated the charts on both sides of the Atlantic the previous year with his 'Stranger On The Shore'. The Beatles recorded this vocal version of 'A Taste Of Honey' no doubt to capitalise on this popularity. Written by American songwriters Bobby Scott and Ric Marlow as a recurring theme for the Broadway production of the play of the same name, the Fabs' version is notable for their first use of a double-tracked vocal – something they were to utilise to great effect over the coming years.

On 'There's A Place', the band's vocal capabilities are further demonstrated, with the composers sharing the lead and Harrison backing them. Liberating the title from Bernstein and Sondheim's 'Somewhere' from the musical *West Side Story*, Lennon declared this song an attempt to capture the *Tamla Motown* sound.

That their influences were largely American can't have harmed their bid for success across the pond, can it?

The album was released the day before American film director and screenwriter Quentin Tarantino was born.

FROM ME TO YOU / THANK YOU GIRL

UK Release: Parlophone R 5015, 11 April 1963 (SP)
Recording data: 5 March 1963, EMI Studios, London
Producer: George Martin
Engineer: Norman Smith

"Our songwriting lifted a little with that song. We were starting to meet other musicians then and we'd start to see other people writing. After that, on another tour bus with Roy Orbison, we saw Roy sitting in the back of the bus, writing 'Pretty Woman'. It was lovely. We could trade off with each other. This was our real start." – **Paul McCartney**

One of the songs that was very much co-written by Lennon and McCartney – at the back of the tour bus near Shrewsbury, apparently. Kenny Lynch tried to help them, but petulantly walked away, declaring the pair "bloody rubbish" songwriters. The title was inspired by the From You To Us letters page of the *New Musical Express*. It was to be the duo's first American hit, but as covered by Del Shannon rather than the Beatles' original recording.

With this song came the full realisation of the band's impact, when McCartney heard his milkman whistling it. And I'm certain that three years later, that very milkman would go on to whistle the Small Faces' 'Sha-La-La-La-Lee' (co-written by Lynch) and drive the fastest milk cart in the west.

Martin had urged the pair to come up with more hits following the success of 'Please Please Me', and initially 'Thank You Girl' was intended to be the follow-up single. But once they'd finished writing 'From Me To You', that song was quickly relegated to the b-side. And it's easy to see why: like the previous two 45s, 'From Me To You' again had the word 'me' in its title. Lennon's use of the old gob-iron was again prevalent on what McCartney would declare a pivotal piece; "our songwriting lifted a little with that song," he said, citing in particular the middle-eight. And this was the song that would cement the falsetto "Whooh!" as a Beatles brand.

Lyrically I was always a little perplexed by the line "I've got arms that long to hold you, and keep you by my side," as one of the arms would have to be incredibly long to achieve this - unless the object of their desire was particularly tiny, I suppose. But writing songs about being beside people can often be troublesome – just look at the Bread song 'If': Lord knows what was David Gates thinking when he wrote "If a man could be two places at one time, I'd be with you tomorrow and today, beside you all the way..." That's one place at two times, right?

The b-side, originally titled 'Thank You, Little Girl', was cunningly written to appeal to their rapidly growing female following.

The recording session for both sides included rehearsals of two songs that would be recorded for later album releases: 'What Goes On' (*Rubber Soul*) and 'One After 909' (*Let It Be*).

Also of interest is the fact that 'From Me To You' marked the last time the writers of a Beatles' record would be listed as McCartney-Lennon. Both the *Please Please Me* album and single were similarly credited, but the next release would revert back to the original 'Love Me Do' format of Lennon-McCartney, which would become the rock 'n' roll brand that McCartney to this day remains proud to have been a part of. And quite rightly so.

This single was released three days after the birth of Lennon's first son, Julian, and was their first bona fide number one, spending seven weeks at the top of the UK chart.

TWIST AND SHOUT

UK Release: Parlophone GEP-8882, 12 July 1963 (EP)
Recording data: 11 February 1963, EMI Studios, London
Producer: George Martin
Engineer: Norman Smith
Tracks: Twist And Shout / A Taste Of Honey / Do You Want To Know A Secret / There's A Place

---

At the time of its release, extended play 45s were still being included in the singles' charts. This EP outsold most 45s for some weeks in 1963, and of course went to number one – despite all of the tracks being culled from the end of the *Please Please Me* long player (the final four tracks, seen? But not necessarily in the right order).

SHE LOVES YOU / I'LL GET YOU

UK Release: Parlophone R 5055, 23 August 1963 (SP)
US Release: Swan S-4152, 16 September 1963 (SP)
Recording data: 1 July 1963, EMI Studios, London
Producer: George Martin
Engineer: Norman Smith

"I remember it was Paul's idea: instead of singing 'I love you' again, we'd have a third party."
- John Lennon

Aside from being the best-selling single of 1963, and still the best-selling Beatles single in Britain to this day, the song is also noteworthy for being the first Beatles recording to be explicitly referenced by the group themselves – Lennon, in fact – during the out-chorus of 'All You Need Is Love', released in July 1967. (It could be argued that 'All You Need Is Love' also includes a mention of the song 'Yesterday', but this is far less overt. Either way, *Wikipedia's* claim that 'Lucy In The Sky With Diamonds' is the first song to be self-referenced is complete and utter wank.) It was also their first single not to feature a harmonica; though Lennon didn't ever fully drop the instrument, he realised it was becoming a bit of a gimmick and so only whipped it out sporadically from hereon in (though it is featured on the b-side).

The song has no bridge, using a refrain to join the verses together. The idea of starting the song with the refrain was George Martin's.

Lennon and McCartney wrote the bulk of the song in the Turk's Hotel, a couple of hours before a show at the Majestic Ballroom in Newcastle-upon-Tyne; they finished it off at Paul's home in Forthlin Road, and performed it for his father, Jim, who was in the living room watching TV.

The song really struck a chord thanks to the recurrence of the now familiar "Whooh!", and the repeated "Yeah! Yeah! Yeah!" phrase - which headline writers around the world quickly seized upon.

The high-energy band performance was down to the fact that fans had infiltrated Abbey Road studios and had been swarming through the building before the band could knuckle down to recording. This undoubtedly helped to ramp up the infectious intensity of what on the face of it is a very simple song.

When engineer Smith first saw the boys' words on the music stand, he thought, "oh my God, what a lyric! This is going to be one that I do not like. But when they started to sing it - bang, wow, terrific." Much like Martin's reaction after they recorded 'Please Please Me', Smith then recognised it as the sure-fire hit it became. With a bullet.

'I'll Get You' (originally designated 'Get You In The End') kept the old conceptual continuity going by repeating the word "yeah", and features unison singing by the songwriters – a characteristic of their early tunes that would lead to confusion about who sang what by some. The opening lyric (after the spiffy handclapped intro) - "Imagine I'm in love with you..." - was also a neat trick to prick up the ears of the listener.

Two days after the single's release, the band played their sixth concert in two months in the seaside town of Blackpool.

THE BEATLES' HITS

UK Release: Parlophone GEP-8880, 6 September 1963 (EP)
Recording data: 1963, EMI Studios, London
Producer: George Martin
Engineer: Norman Smith
Tracks: From Me to You / Thank You Girl / Please Please Me / Love Me Do

---

Another shameless 'greatest hits' cash-in which went to number one in the UK singles' chart. Released in mono only, sports' fans.

EMI had of course cottoned on to the fact that the kids were now buying anything with The Beatles' mugs on, even recordings they already owned, and so issued a run of similar extended players for the next few years.

George at De Montfort Hall, Leicester, 1 December 1963. Practising Paul's parts just in case?
© Richard Mitchell / Rex

THE BEATLES (NO. 1)

UK Release: Parlophone GEP-8883, 6 September 1963 (EP)
Recording data: 11 February 1963, EMI Studios, London
Producer: George Martin
Engineer: Norman Smith
Tracks: I Saw Her Standing There / Misery / Anna (Go To Him) / Chains

---

Another cash-in, but now the fans were getting wise: this compilation of the first four songs from the *Please Please Me* album (in the self-same running order – so that now only 'Boys' and 'Baby It's You' had not made it onto a 45rpm record in this country) only went to number two in the UK singles' chart. Number 2 - pah! That'll learn 'em.

Again, released solely in mono. The cover uses an alternative image from sessions for the *Please Please Me* album artwork.

WITH THE BEATLES (BEATLEMANIA! WITH THE BEATLES)*

UK Release: Parlophone PMC 1206 (mono) / PCS 3045 (stereo), 22 November 1963 (LP)
*Canadian Release: Capitol Canada Capitol T-6051, 25 November 1963 (LP)
Recording data: 18 July – 23 October 1963, EMI Studios, London
Producer: George Martin
Engineer: Norman Smith
Tracks: It Won't Be Long / All I've Got To Do / All My Loving / Don't Bother Me / Little Child / Till There Was You / Please Mister Postman / Roll Over Beethoven / Hold Me Tight / You Really Gotta Hold On Me / I Wanna Be Your Man / Devil In Her Heart / Not A Second Time / Money.

"The first album was really a recital of their repertoire. With The Beatles was the first songbook, so to speak." – **George Martin**

This album knocked *Please Please Me* from the top of the UK album charts and ensured that the band were number one for 51 consecutive weeks. That's nearly a year, yeah? Yeah! Yeah? Yeah! Yeah? Yeah! Kind of ironic that the first track is 'It Won't Be Long' then, eh? And what a fantastic opener. Stylistically similar to 'From Me To You' but performed with more vigour. This was the first original recorded for the album (on 30 July 1963) and it set the bar pretty high.

Martin says that at this point the band were still thinking in terms of issuing singles and *With The Beatles* comprises the songs that weren't considered good enough to be 45s – performed by the Beatles, that is. And that is quite something when you consider that this album includes sing-along gems like 'All My Loving' and the afore-mentioned 'It Won't Be Long'. And that Starr was still warbling the song Lennon and McCartney gifted to the Rolling Stones ('I Wanna Be Your Man') at the time of the band's last live concert three years later. It just proves that a Beatles throwaway is another band's treasure, I guess.

In his marvellously enlightening tome, *Life*, Keith Richards reveals how Andrew Loog Oldham became The Rolling Stones' manager/producer after getting into a "bitch argument" with Epstein, for whom he worked (with the Beatles) in early 1963. The Stones were having trouble coming up with a follow-up song to their debut single, a cover of Chuck Berry's 'Come On'. Oldham later threatened to lock Richards and lead vocalist Mick Jagger in a room until they came up with original material, but before then he bumped into Lennon and McCartney in Charing Cross Road. The pair had just left a luncheon at the Savoy Hotel where they had received an award for Top Vocal Group Of The Year from the Variety Club of Great Britain. Oldham told them of his dilemma. Continues Richards, "They came back to the studio with him and gave us a song that was on their next album but wasn't coming out as a single, 'I Wanna Be Your Man'. They played it through with us. Brian [Jones] put on some nice slide guitar; we turned it into an unmistakably Stones rather than Beatles song. It was clear that we had a hit almost before they'd left the studio."

McCartney admitted the Stones "Bo Diddleyed" up a song Lennon would later dismiss as "throwaway" – adding, "We weren't going to give them anything great!"

As most people know, there was (and to some extent, still is) a rivalry between Beatles and Stones fans. The reality of course was that the musicians themselves were quite matey. Here's an extract from a chat between McCartney and Harrison that appeared in the June 1966 edition of *The Beatles Monthly*:
George: There's a rumour going round that the Rolling Stones will retire if the Beatles get to number one with 'Paperback Writer'.

Paul: Yes, Mick told me so himself. I think he said they'd retire in 1997.
George: Good, I'll record 'Paint It, Black' as a multi-tracked sitar solo in 1998 for our Christmas fan club record. And you can hold me to that!

Of course, Harrison never kept his promise and the Stones continue to perform to this day (as does McCartney who, in issue 41 of said fanzine, is quoted as saying, "We'd hate to be touring when we're thirty-five, because we'd look silly... probably bald when we're thirty.")

'All My Loving', although never ever a single in the UK (but a number one in Canada), should be familiar to one and all right to this very day – you'll hear it in your local *Morrisons*. Go visit, and hang around in Market Street checking out their fine produce for a while. Unusually for McCartney, he wrote the lyrics first, and the music second. Lennon admitted it was one of his partner's finest efforts, and responded by adding some splendid background licks, while Harrison's country and western flavoured guitar solo elevated the song yet further.

'Till There Was You' was written by Meredith Willson for the 1957 musical, The Music Man. McCartney though was more familiar with Peggy Lee's version, and thought the inclusion of this 'offbeat' tune in the band's repertoire "showed that we weren't just another rock 'n' roll group". Although it had been in the band's act since 1962 - and was part of their failed *Decca* audition - they previewed it for the nation during the Royal Command Performance at the London's Prince of Wales Theatre on 4 November, in the presence of the Queen Mum and Princess Margaret.

In his memoir, *A Cellarful Of Noise*, Brian Epstein recalls that he detected a flaw in McCartney's vocal during the song. Lennon was "abominally rude" to him, telling his manager loudly, "We'll make the record. You just go on counting your percentages."

'Hold Me Tight' was originally recorded during that marathon session of 11 February 1963 for the *Please Please Me* album, but the band was unsatisfied with their performance and binned it – literally. They re-recorded it seven months later for this album, and were obviously happier this time around. The song had been a part of their live set since McCartney wrote it two years earlier.

With The Beatles featured Harrison's first ever recorded solo composition ('Don't Bother Me'), which proved that he could, if he persisted, do it - although he didn't get another song on an album for a couple of years. But he did get to sing lead vocals on two other songs on here, as well as sharing lead vocal duties with Lennon on another (Smokey Robinson's 'You Really Got A Hold On Me'). Lennon and McCartney penned half of the songs. Of the covers, three come from Motown, the inclusion of which would lead to many a youngster becoming soul aficionados.

Sincerely. I actually know someone who got turned onto soul music because of this album. He then became all snooty after hearing 'Please Mr. Postman' by The Marvelettes, totally dismissing the lads for ripping off the Tamla sound. But the fact is, through the Beatles many thousands got to hear music they never would have, and for that we should be grateful.

It's just not the same today when music is far more readily accessible, and straight covers of old songs – like Paloma Faith's almost faithful rendition of INXS's 'Never Tear Us Apart', for example – serve no purpose other than to make a quick buck (either for the artist or, in the case quoted, suppliers of haberdashery and household goods). The Beatles were playing songs they actually studied and wanted to play and have people hear, to show off their great taste.

And as for the Marvelettes, they had 'Please Mr. Postman' crafted for them by at least three songwriters, and then played and arranged by the legendary Funk Brothers. What the Beatles alone went on to do with their own compositions warrants far greater respect. And while inspiring those that maybe found the band's early work a little 'flimsy' to seek out music they'd stick with for life, those of us who hung on in there would also later be pointed towards classical and so-called world music, as well as many other life enhancing riches. Dig out your soul records, and you'll find covers of Beatles songs by the likes of Otis Redding, Stevie Wonder, Ray Charles, Arthur Conley, Diana Ross and Earth, Wind & Fire. Yes, there really can be no argument that the Beatles were the most influential rock and roll band ever.

Another motor city hit on *With The Beatles* was 'Money (That's What I Want)', written by Tamla founder Berry Gordy with Janie Bradford, and recorded by Barrett Strong. In a bid to emulate the thrilling denouement of their debut album, Lennon sang his Chelsea boots off over this piano pounder. Simple but effective.

With The Beatles' black and white front cover photograph of the boys half-shaded heads was taken by Robert Freeman, who was to photograph and design the covers for the group's next four consecutive UK albums (as well as Lennon's first two books). *Parlophone* deemed the artwork "shockingly humourless", but it's a measure of the band's clout this early in their career that they were able to stand their ground and keep this now iconic cover.

Beatlemania – an expression coined by the *Daily Mirror* on 14 October following the group's appearance on the popular and influential TV variety show *Sunday Night At The London Palladium* – was now in full swing in the UK where it was hard to avoid these platters; they were being "spun pon de replay" at all the best house parties while teenagers avidly pored over every word of Tony Barrow's sleeve notes. (Barrow was the band's press officer from 1962 to 1968, and was the man who thunked up the phrase 'The Fab Four'.)

Between the release of the *Please Please Me* album and this follow-up, the UK Government came a-tumbling down as a result of its Defence Secretary having had an affair with 'party girl' Christine Keeler. Having denied any wrongdoing to Parliament in the March, John Profumo (for it was he) admitted two months later that he had in fact misled the House and did the decent thing. It is believed that this scandal impacted on the health of then Prime Minister Harold Macmillan, who himself stood down in October and then saw the Conservative party lose power a year later, having been in office since 1951.

In May, the last National Servicemen left the UK Armed Forces - a not insignificant factor in the changes that were about to happen: a nation of men who were used to following rules would soon start questioning the status quo, and be happy for their wives and servants to read D. H. Lawrence's *Lady Chatterley's Lover*.

This was indeed a period of great turmoil and change for the Western world: in July 1963, the Moors murderers claimed their first victim; in August, the Great Train Robbery took place, Martin Luther King delivered his 'I Have A Dream' speech, and Todd Carty was born. And as if all of that wasn't enough, on the very day that *With The Beatles* was released, US President John F Kennedy was assassinated in Dallas, Texas.

I WANT TO HOLD YOUR HAND / THIS BOY

UK Release: Parlophone R 5084, 29 November 1963 (SP)
Recording data: 17 October 1963, EMI Studios, London
Producer: George Martin
Engineer: Norman Smith

"I remember when we got the chord that made the song. We were in Jane Asher's house, downstairs in the cellar playing on the piano at the same time. And we had, 'Oh you-u-u... got that something...' And Paul hits this chord and I turn to him and say, 'That's it!' I said, 'Do that again!' In those days, we really used to absolutely write like that - both playing into each other's nose." – **John Lennon**

Okay, this is quite possibly why I'm writing all this old tosh. 'I Want To Hold Your Hand' was the first record this author ever bought. Fact. But it oh so easily could've been Frank Ifield's 'I Remember You', a year earlier (a song, incidentally, that the Beatles would also perform in 1962– viz.: *Live! At The Star-Club In Hamburg, Germany; 1962*). But it wasn't, I held out for something a little more enduring and the first pennies of my unearned pocket money spent on vinyl were for this recording.

Yet another example of two quality songs, recorded in one day and released a mere several weeks later, not allowing any dust to settle after the release of *With The Beatles*. The song was written in the basement of McCartney's actress girlfriend Jane Asher's home. Her brother Peter (of Peter And Gordon and James Taylor fame) said, "My mother had a practice room that she used to give private oboe lessons when she wasn't teaching at The Royal Academy, where she was a professor. There was just a piano, and an upright chair and a sofa. Paul used that room to write in, from time to time. One afternoon John came over, while I was upstairs in my room. The two of them were in the basement for an hour or so, and Paul called me down to listen to a song they had just finished. I went downstairs and sat on the sofa, and they sat side by side, on the piano bench. That's where they played 'I Want to Hold Your Hand' for the first time anywhere. They asked me what I thought. I said, 'I think it's very good'!"

'I Want To Hold Your Hand' was released as a single in the US, with 'I Saw Her Standing There' on the b-side. It reached the top of the charts there in February 1964, the month the band famously played on The Ed Sullivan Show on three consecutive Sundays. In fact, this was the song that Epstein had been waiting for to conquer America. He'd turned down a previous offer to appear on the show but, on hearing this, knew immediately it was the right record with which to assault the States.

Having dismissed a high sum for a one-off show, Epstein insisted on a much smaller amount for the three shows. His gamble paid off, and Beatlemania gripped the States big time.

Their first Sullivan appearance on 9 February had an estimated 73 million viewers, setting a new record for US television - as well as seeing a temporary drop in the crime rate in the country!

McCartney subsequently commented that people talked about it like a 'where were you when Kennedy was shot' moment. Interestingly, because of such comparisons, the Beatles declined a ticker tape parade when they returned in August for their first full US tour.

B-side 'This Boy' is a ballad considered strong enough to be played during their second Sullivan show TV appearance. Of its composition, McCartney said, "We weren't all rock 'n' roll, we could change the pace, which was always nice after you'd played for three hours. We wrote it in two-part harmony and then put the third part in for George to sing; we'd never actually tried to write something like that. Nice middle, John sang that great, then we'd go back into the close-harmony thing." The harmony vocals were double-tracked and pretty damn lush.

Lennon viewed it as an attempt at writing a doo-wop type Smokey Robinson song, and later said, "There was a period when I thought I didn't write melodies, that Paul wrote those and I just wrote straight, shouting rock 'n' roll. But of course, when I think of some of my own songs - [like] 'This Boy' - I was writing melody with the best of them."

THE BEATLES' CHRISTMAS RECORD

UK Release: Lyntone LYN 492, 6 December 1963 (SP)
Recording data: 17 October 1963, Dick James Music, London
Producer: Tony Barrow

The first of seven 'not for sale' singles issued free to members of the group's official fan-club in the UK at Christmas time. These were the brain-child of Barrow, who foresaw a PR disaster looming as the team running the fan-club struggled to cope with the huge volume of mail being sent to the band.

Epstein initially dismissed this damage limitation exercise, but the boys loved the idea and asked Barrow to prepare a script. Epstein's concern revolved around the fact that the fan-club was a non-profit making affair and he would inevitably have to subsidise such a venture. Looking at ways to keep costs down, Barrow therefore approached *Lyntone Records*, who produced flexi-discs for *Reader's Digest* to promote its new classical album sets.

In his memoir, John, Paul, George, Ringo And Me, Barrow also cites as an influence the flexi-discs occasionally issued by fortnightly satirical magazine *Private Eye*. While *Lyntone* did indeed produce these 'cover-mounts' for them, the first one didn't come out until October 1964. Bing!

An interesting observation here is that in the three books written by three of the band's inner circle during their most popular phase – that is, Tony Barrow, Alistair Taylor and Peter Brown (another of Epstein's personal assistants, and an executive director of NEMS) – neither has very much to say about the others. It's hard to believe that their paths hardly crossed, but maybe their respective books' Fab-centric focus left little time for reminiscences about the supporting cast. For the record, Barrow makes less than a half dozen comments about Taylor and none about Brown, while Taylor mentions Barrow just the once. When Taylor passed away in 2004, Barrow did though describe him as "a wonderful number two" - like one that you get naked for, I imagine. As for Brown, he's comparatively effusive about the other two, while Taylor describes his book (*The Love You Make: An Insider's Story Of The Beatles*, co-written with Steve Gaines) as "appalling". Ouch!

So it would seem it wasn't just the Fab Four that fell out in the end. Anyway, the Christmas records included messages of thanks to loyal Beatle 'peedles' (German slang for penis, apparently), skits, carols and - later - original compositions. None have ever been subject to general release, though an edited chunkette did appear as part of the Anthology project... keep reading!

Barrow says he and Paul S. Lynton (founder of *Lyntone*) hurriedly edited together – with a pair of scissors – the boys' greetings, and now ponders the value of the pieces of tape that littered the floor before being swept away never to be heard again.

Eagle-eyed readers will note that this was taped the same day the boys laid down 'I Want To Hold Your Hand' and 'This Boy'.

INTRODUCING... THE BEATLES

US Release: Vee-Jay SR-1062, 10 January 1964 (LP)
Recording data: 11 September and 26 November 1962, 11 & 20 February 1963, EMI Studios, London
Producer: George Martin
Engineer: Norman Smith
Tracks: I Saw Her Standing There / Misery / Anna (Go To Him) / Chains / Boys / Love Me Do / P.S. I Love You / Baby It's You / Do You Want To Know A Secret / A Taste Of Honey / There's A Place / Twist And Shout

---

Upon release of its 'Please Please Me' single in the US, *Vee-Jay Records* signed a licensing agreement with *Transglobal* (an *EMI* owned company) that gave it first dibs on future Beatles' recordings. The label was sent the masters for the *Please Please Me* album, but plans for a US release were abandoned when the company got into financial difficulties (in part caused by the company president's gambling debts). As a consequence, *Vee-Jay* decided not to report royalties on sales of its Beatles records released thus far (including those issued by its subsidiary, *Tollie Records*) and *Transglobal* declared its contract with the label null and void. When *Vee-Jay* then got wind of *Capitol's* big plans for new Beatles recordings, it reviewed the material it had in its vaults and, in a bold shit-or bust move, released this version of *Introducing... The Beatles.*

Following a restraining order from *Capitol Records*, an *EMI* label in the States, the album was withdrawn one month after release and immediately replaced with a version that swapped 'Love Me Do' and 'P.S. I Love You' – two songs effectively owned by *Capitol* – for 'Ask Me Why' and 'Please Please Me'.

Capitol again tried to stop *Vee-Jay* releasing a Beatles album in any form, taking the company to court on numerous occasions. Finally, the two labels reached a settlement that allowed *Vee-Jay* to issue the 16 Beatles' songs it controlled in any way it chose until 15 October 1964. After that date, all rights in the US reverted to *Capitol*... but *Vee-Jay* managed to sell over one million copies of its different versions of *Introducing... The Beatles.*

MEET THE BEATLES!

US Release: Capitol ST-2047, 20 January 1964 (LP)
Recording data: 11 February – 23 October 1963, EMI Studios, London
Producer: George Martin
Engineer: Norman Smith
Tracks: I Want To Hold Your Hand / I Saw Her Standing There / This Boy / It Won't Be Long / All I've Got To Do / All My Loving / Don't Bother Me / Little Child / Till There Was You / Hold Me Tight / I Wanna Be Your Man / Not A Second Time

---

The second US album, released just ten days after the first on a different label but replicating one track. By 13 March, it had sold over 3,600,000 copies, making it the then biggest selling album of all time.

New series—the PEOPLE behind the BEATLES—1

BRIAN EPSTEIN

By CHRIS HUTCHINS

A YEAR ago this week the Beatles' "Please Please Me" blasted to No. 1 in the NME Chart. It was their first chart-topper and manager Brian Epstein took the foursome to an Italian restaurant in Soho to celebrate the achievement.

No one recognised the four rather strange looking boys with their Stone Age hairstyles and Chelsea boots, for Beatlemania had still to make its marked impression on the world.

Last week red-headed Cilla Black soared to the top spot with "Anyone Who Had A Heart" and Brian launched his twelfth "No. 1 celebration party" in a year — no less than eleven discs by his artists ("She Loves You" did it twice) have bounded into the chart in twelve months.

A further four discs by stars from his stable have been smash hits.

At 29 this rather shy young manager with the boyish looking face has climbed to the very top of the music business ladder with a trail of major successes that would take a column to list.

Actor

Brian Epstein wanted to be an actor but his father was keen to see him enter the family furnishing business. So when Brian left Wrekin College in Shropshire at the early age of 16, he began a five-year furniture salesman apprenticeship at £5 a week.

But at 21 his love of the theatre diverted him to the Royal Academy of Dramatic Art, where he pursued his first love, the theatre, for eighteen months before returning to the family's Liverpool store.

The story of how he found the Beatles virtually on his own doorstep in Liverpool is now history. From their initial, though modest, success with "Love Me Do," Epstein has never looked back.

He launched Gerry and the Pacemakers, Billy J. Kramer and the Dakotas, the Fourmost and Cilla Black, all of whom were to repeat the "particularly happy moment" which he experiences every time one of them breaks into the chart with a new hit or sends box office bookings soaring with the news that they're coming to town."

BRIAN EPSTEIN

But not all of Brian's experiences in the past year have been those "particularly happy" ones.

His amiable nature, tempered with a slight inferiority complex, lends itself easily to embarrassment and the blushes reporters love to write about.

One such experience happened as the Beatles were half-way through one of their earliest recording sessions. Brian criticised a track they had just taped.

"Listen, we'll make the records—you just count the percentage," retorted John Lennon angrily in front of recording manager and engineers.

"Believe it or not, that was one of the most embarrassing moments in my career," Brian told me, quivering slightly at the memory of it.

But Brian need not have worried. This youthful and dedicated manager with the golden touch has the respect of all his artists, and by making such an open retort at the session John Lennon was emphasising the close and frank relationship that exists between Epstein and all his stars.

The well-spoken ex-RADA student who also once had a yen to take up dress-designing—is very different to many of his contemporaries, such as Elvis Presley's manager, Colonel Tom Parker.

Until pop music became his life, Brian was more at home with classical music, though at about the time he entered RADA he "seems to remember liking 'Baby Face' by Little Richard."

With the Beatles' major American success, appearances by most of his artists on the Palladium TV show, and Cilla Black's booking for a London Palladium season already achieved, Brian's ambitions now veer back towards a personal theatrical career.

He is anxious to present, produce and direct a play in the West End—and possibly to act in one.

Jury

Tomorrow evening Epstein makes his second appearance on "Juke Box Jury." He could have made several more in recent months but always needs persuasion to enter the limelight.

He even refuses to answer personally the fan mail which pours in for him daily. "I believe the fans should be for my artists—not for me," he says firmly.

Pressmen track his movements at all times and the telephone in his Knightsbridge flat rarely stops ringing, even late at night, for he believes in taking every decision of any importance in connection with NEMS Enterprises, personally.

Though now one of the most sought after men in the London social world, the young bachelor dislikes parties and social functions. Despite his solid business dealings he is often stumped for words at such occasions.

The company he likes best is that of his artists. With all of them he enjoys the friendly relationship that goes from building a career alongside them.

ALL MY LOVING

UK Release: Parlophone GEP-8891, 7 February 1964 (EP)
Recording data: 1963, EMI Studios, London
Producer: George Martin
Engineer: Norman Smith
Tracks: All My Loving / Ask Me Why / Money (That's What I Want) / P.S. I Love You

---

Did *EMI* have no shame? A fourth British EP compiling four songs - two of which were the b-sides of their first two singles (with the other two from their current album). Come on!

And yet still it sold: number one for eight weeks. In fairness, 'All My Loving' was worthy of being a hit single, and I guess the girlies were quite content with 7 rather than 12 inches. Fnarr!

Again, released solely in mono. The cover uses an alternate version of the Robert Freeman image from the *With The Beatles* sleeve.

Latest Beatlemania report from New York—

NOW A GOLD DISC FOR BEATLES' U.S. ALBUM

SALES WORTH MORE THAN ONE MILLION DOLLARS HAVE BEEN ACHIEVED BY THE BEATLES' CAPITOL ALBUM, WINNING THEM ANOTHER GOLD DISC IN AMERICA—JUST TWO AND A HALF WEEKS AFTER ITS RELEASE THERE. BY AMERICAN RULES THE ALBUM QUALIFIES FOR SUCH AN AWARD WHEN THE COMPANY HAS NETTED A MILLION DOLLARS FROM HALF THE RETAIL PRICE OF THE RECORD. BY WEDNESDAY CAPITOL HAD SOLD 850,000 COPIES OF THE CHART-TOPPING LP, CABLES NAT HENTOFF.

● The Beatles' headlining spot on the "Ed Sullivan Show" this Sunday will now be the first of three consecutive appearances they are to make on America's top TV programme, for the insert they telerecord directly after will be slotted in on February 23. As previously reported they co-star with Mitzi Gaynor when the show is televised direct from Miami on February 16.

● More than 50,000 requests for tickets to the studio, where the Beatles will televise from in the "Ed Sullivan Show" on Sunday, have been received by CBS. This is an even greater demand than CBS had for tickets when Elvis Presley starred in the show at a similar stage in his career. The studio seats just 1,500.

● In next week's "Billboard" chart the Beatles' positions are as follows: No. 1 "I Want To Hold Your Hand"; No. 3 "She Loves You"; No. 45 "Please Please Me"; No. 54 "I Saw Her Standing There" and No. 67 "My Bonnie." "From Me To You" has slipped out although it figures in the "Cash Box" Top Hundred at No. 73. As predicted last week Swan is preparing a Gold Disc for "She Loves You" expecting it to exceed sales of one million this weekend.

CARNEGIE DISC

Parlophone a-and-r chief George Martin is now certain to record their Carnegie Hall concert next Wednesday for an American album. Although several of the songs are likely to have been previously issued in America, Capitol considers that the Beatles appearance at the Hall is of sufficient importance to justify the LP. It may not be issued in Britain.

Two American records, inspired by the Beatles' phenomenal success in America, are issued here by Pye on Tuesday. They are "The Boy With The Beatle Hair," by the Swans on Cameo Parkway, and "A Beatle I Want To Be," by Sonny Curtis (of the Crickets) on Colpix.

Newly issued in America is an album, "Beatle Mania In The U.S.A.", by a group called the Liverpools and an instrumental single, "The Beatles" by another American group, the Buddies.

KOMM, GIB MIR DEINE HAND / SIE LIEBT DICH

German Release: Odeon Records, 5 March 1964 (SP)
Recording data: 29 January 1964, Pathé Marconi Studios, Paris
Producer: George Martin
Engineer: Norman Smith

Odeon Records, the German sub-label of *EMI*, came up with the idea of the band recording German language versions of 'I Want to Hold Your Hand' and 'She Loves You', "so that they could sell more records there." The Beatles were on tour in France at the time, and were about to record 'Can't Buy Me Love' in Paris (the band's only recording session outside of London). They agreed to go along with this scam.

The lyrics were translated by Camillo Felgen, a Luxembourgian singer and television presenter, who flew to Paris to teach the band the versions phonetically in the studio.

The vocals for 'Komm, Gib Mir Deine Hand' were recorded first, then mixed with the original instrumental backing track, with handclaps overdubbed

Amazingly, the original recording of 'She Loves You' had been destroyed by *EMI*, so the band had to re-record 'Sie Liebt Dich' from scratch.

Save for, notably, Johnny Cash, David Bowie and Peter Gabriel, re-recording songs in a Teutonic language is not something many others artists have attempted since. I can't imagine why not.

Or can I? Perhaps this old adage will help: "Tell someone you love them today, because life is short. But shout it at them in German, because life is also terrifying!"

'Sie Liebt Dich' was released as a single in the United States, with the original 'She Loves You' b-side - 'I'll Get You' - on the b-side.

BEATLES U.S. SHOW MADE INTO FILM

THE BEATLES occupy both first and second positions in "Billboard's" American chart next week. Their Washington concert will be shown in cinemas throughout American next month.

The group will play Scarborough Futurist on Sunday, July 12. They will be followed on successive Sundays at the venue by the Searchers, Gerry and the Pacemakers and Brian Poole and the Tremeloes.

In the U.S. trade magazine "Billboard" next week, "I Want To Hold Your Hand" is No. 1 and "She Loves You" is No. 2, cables Nat Hentoff. "Please Please Me" is No. 29, "I Saw Her Standing There" (35) and "My Bonnie" (54).

The Beatles broke a television viewing record for New York City on Sunday night. Nearly 75 per cent. of the sets being used at the time of the show were tuned in to the group. However, reviews of the programme were mild.

The Beatles received two Capitol Gold Discs at their Press conference on Monday (see picture on page 3). They were also presented with one from Swan for "She Loves You" on Wednesday, cables Chris Hutchins.

The Washington concert by the group was video-taped on Tuesday night and will be shown by closed-circuit television in cinemas throughout the U.S. on March 21-22.

Their Carnegie Hall concert on Wednesday could not be recorded for an LP as planned owing to an objection by the American Federation of Musicians.

Stop press Beatle news—

BBC-TV TO FILM BEATLES RETURN FROM STATES

THE BEATLES' return to London tomorrow (Saturday) morning will be filmed by a BBC-TV unit for transmission a few hours later. John, Paul, Ringo and George will headline a marathon radio show on Easter Monday. The screening date for a television show in which they star has been fixed.

THE BEATLES arrive back at London airport from their sensationally successful U.S. trip at 7.40 am tomorrow. BBC-TV's Outside Broadcast programme "Grandstand" will cover the arrival of their Pan-American flight. It will be screened at 1 pm tomorrow.

The programme will include interviews with fans waiting on the roof of the terminal building and a commentary from the reception hall when the Beatles step inside.

THE BEATLES top the bill in a special two-hour Light Programme presentation on Easter Monday, March 30 (10 am—noon). It will be similar in format to the one in which they starred on Boxing Day morning.

The Swinging Blue Jeans have also been booked for the show and other pop stars are being sought.

THE BEATLES' edition of ATV's recorded "Morecambe And Wise" show series will be screened on April 18, it was revealed to the NME on Wednesday.

THE BEATLES' arrival by riverboat at ABC-TV's Teddington Studios on Sunday will be filmed as the opening setting for the edition of "Big Night Out" in which they star the following Saturday (29th). (London viewers will, of course, see "Bonanza" when viewers in other regions receive the show).

THE BEATLES have been voted winners of the "Show Business Personality" Award by the Variety Club of Great Britain. Cliff Richard, Frankie Vaughan, Max Bygraves, Lionel Bart, Harry Secombe and Billy Cotton have all held the title in previous years.

British discs still top in America

THE BEATLES now have three singles in America's Top Ten! Their "Meet The Beatles" album has sold more than 1,600,000 copies and is expected to be the first LP to sell two million in Capitol's history. But they are not the only British recording artists making an impression on the U.S. charts.

In next week's "Cash Box" "I Want To Hold Your Hand" remains No. 1 and Capitol says that present sales of well over 2,500,000 may reach the three-and-a-half-million mark.

"She Loves You" stays at No. 2 in next week's charts, and "Please Please Me" enters at No. 10 with "My Bonny" rising 10 places to No. 39.

Dusty Springfield's "I Only Want To Be With You" will be No. 15, the Dave Clark Five's "Glad All Over" No. 33, and Cliff Richard's "It's All In The Game" slips after a long period to No. 40.

A new British entry is the Searchers' "Needles And Pins" which bows the group into the Top Hundred at No. 80.

● Beatles' discs are currently topping the charts in four other countries—"I Want To Hold Your Hand" in Holland, New Zealand and Norway, and "I Saw Her Standing There" in Australia.

NEW BEATLES DISC

THE BEATLES' next single is called "Can't Buy Me Love," and will be issued on March 20. The disc couples two more Paul McCartney-John Lennon compositions—the flipside is "You Can't Do That" . . . Next week, the Beatles top the U.S. charts with "I Want To Hold Your Hand" for the sixth successive week; "She Loves You" remains at No. 2, "Please Please Me" rises another six places to No. 4, "Standing There" is No. 18 and "My Bonnie" No. 32. Their "Twist And Shout" single enters the "Cash Box" Hundred at No. 64.

London viewers will see Beatles 'Big Night Out'

VIEWERS in every ITV region will be able to see the Beatles edition of ABC-TV's "Big Night Out" after all! This week the programme companies for London and the South of England both agreed to start showing the highly rated pop series—but on different nights.

Elsewhere on the network, viewers will see the show tomorrow (Saturday)—but London pop fans will see it on Tuesday at 8 pm, and Southern viewers on March 27.

After next week's edition, the London company will show the series four days in advance of the network on Tuesday evenings, while Southern will screen editions four weeks after the rest of Britain, commencing with the Beatles show on Good Friday.

The show starring Adam Faith, the Roulettes, Patsy Ann Noble and Margo Henderson will be transmitted in London on Tuesday, March 10, and by the remainder of Britain (except Southern-TV) on Saturday (14th).

A switch in bookings means that the King Brothers, Des O'Connor and Joyce Blair will now be featured in the following show (London, March 17, remainder March 21).

Other bookings include Susan Maughan (London 24th, rest 28th), Diana Dors (London 31st, rest April 4), and Kathy Kirby (London 7th, rest 11th).

Beatles revival

AN instrumental recorded by the Beatles two years ago is a surprise release on Polydor today (Friday). The number, "Cry For A Shadow," was written by George Harrison and John Lennon and features the group's former drummer Pete Best.

Tony Sheridan sings "Why" (a number he penned with Bill Crompton) backed by the Beatles on the flip-side.

CAN'T BUY ME LOVE / YOU CAN'T DO THAT

UK Release: Parlophone R 5114, 16 March 1964 (SP)
Recording data: 29 January 1964, Pathé Marconi Studios, Paris; 25 February 1964, EMI Studios, London.
Producer: George Martin
Engineers: Norman Smith and Geoff Emerick

"I thought that we really needed a tag for the song's ending, and a tag for the beginning; a kind of intro. So I took the first two lines of the chorus and changed the ending, and said 'Let's just have these lines, and by altering the second phrase we can get back into the verse pretty quickly.'" And they said, 'That's not a bad idea, we'll do it that way.'" – **George Martin**

The second record I ever owned – well, the first that I co-owned: my father and grandfather bought this single for my brother and I! At the time of writing, I still have that very piece of plastic in my home. In the loft.

'Can't Buy Me Love' was both written and primarily recorded in Paris, and was the first single solely sung by one singer: McCartney, the main composer. When they bought the initial recording back to Abbey Road, Emerick says, "the tape had a ripple in it, resulting in the intermittent loss of treble on Ringo's hi-hat cymbal... the Beatles themselves were unavailable, so George and Norman took it upon themselves to make a little adjustment. As I eagerly headed into the engineer's seat for the first time, Norman headed down into the studio to overdub a hastily set-up hi-hat onto a few bars of the song while I recorded him."

McCartney was appalled that the lyrics had been interpreted by some as a song of praise to a prostitute, and clarified that, "The idea behind it was that all these material possessions are all very well, but they won't buy me what I really want."

Written in the immediate aftermath of the soaraway success of 'I Want To Hold Your Hand', the boys felt obligated to come up with something equally stellar. Their fourth single proper reached number one in the UK and was their third to sell over a million copies.

'You Can't Do That' was Lennon's "attempt at being Wilson Pickett" and was the first song by the band on which he played lead guitar. It also was the first set of lyrics

the author ever completely memorised, but please don't ask him to sing it, as he probably will!

The song is notable for being the first release on which Harrison's newly acquired *Rickenbacker 360/12* guitar is clearly audible - a distinctive and hugely influential sound. The guitar – the second one ever manufactured by *Rickenbacker* - was gifted to Harrison by Francis C. Hall of the company when the boys were in New York in February 1964; a cute move that would both rocket sales of *Rickenbackers* and change the sound of The Beatles. Frankie say: "Yay!"

In April 1964, during this release's second week at number one in the US charts, the Beatles had fourteen songs on the Hot 100 at the same time.
The world was now officially their lobster.

Cordell Marks talks with singer TONY SHERIDAN about

The hard-up days of the Beatles

ANTHONY ESMOND SHERIDAN McGINNITY poised his tea cup in mid-air and looked reflective. Anthony, ex-art school student from Norwich, known to friends and fans alike as Tony Sheridan, was talking of his days with the Beatles and of how a record with those same boys playing the backing, came to be born.

The record is Polydor's "My Bonnie," which has just netted considerable sales in the States on the MGM label and put up a fair, if so far unastounding, showing over here.

"Life," said Tony "is beginning to get hectic and that's the way I like it."

Aged 23, he looks like a sophisticated Beatle. He has the same hairstyle, though it is considerably shorter and tinged with grey. "I don't know why. I seldom worry, yet it is getting worse." And he wears a grey jacket — with collar — and an old school tie.

We were sitting in a Denmark Street coffee bar.

"Oh yes, I remember meeting the Beatles for the first time. That was in 1961. I was singing at the Top Ten club in Hamburg. I used to join in with all the groups and then one day this new crowd arrived. They were dressed in leather jackets and tight jeans, and looked like initiated 'teds'!

TONY SHERIDAN holds up a picture of the Beatles.

"Stuart Sutcliffe, who died in April, 1962, was with them then, and Pete Best was on drums. John, Paul and George made up the rest of the group.

"I did the singing and they backed me up. Life was one long, long rave from night till morning. Those haircuts? Well, when they first arrived in Germany they all had ordinary short hairstyles, but money was tight and no one wanted to waste money on trivialities. So the hair just grew!

Attic

"We all lived in an attic above the club. Bare boards, freezing drafts, the lot! Bit like Oliver Twist! There were bunk beds. John use to have the top bunk and he'd crash around when he got up because he could never see a thing without his glasses.

"Once he started banging around we all had to get up. John was a wild character in those days.

"The others were a little quieter, but there wasn't much in it. They were all ravers! Yet during all the time out there in Hamburg there was never any thought of making the big time. We were there for the kicks and the laughs—and we got plenty of those"!

He put down the cup and returned the cool blue-eyed stare that was coming his way from the girl at the corner table.

"Our day began at about two in the afternoon, when we would swagger down to the Seamen's Mission for a meal. I don't know why but we always used to have the same meal. All the time, everywhere. Tea and cornflakes. Or sometimes we'd vary it and have cornflakes and tea!

Go, go!

"Then we'd meet our friends and go down to the club and do the stint. Sometimes it would last six hours or more. What a jumping place that was. Go, go, go, there all the time!

"One day, however, things did actually stop. Pete Best and I had been arguing music policy for some

THE BEATLES' SECOND ALBUM

US Release: Capitol ST-2080, 10 April 1964 (LP)
Recording data: 5 & 13 March; 1, 18 & 30 July, 17 October 1963; 25 February & 1 March 1964, EMI Studios, London
Producer: George Martin
Engineer: Norman Smith
Tracks: Roll Over Beethoven / Thank You Girl / You Really Got a Hold on Me / Devil in Her Heart / Money (That's What I Want) / You Can't Do That / Long Tall Sally / I Call Your Name / Please Mister Postman / I'll Get You / She Loves You

---

With the States now very much in catch-up mode, the band's third US album in four months managed to scoop the UK by including one unreleased song (albeit a cover, 'Long Tall Sally' would not debut on a UK release for another couple of months). The album title was also an attempt by *Capitol* to piss over *Vee-Jay's* million selling efforts with the first US album. What larks.

© David Magnus / Rex

AIN'T SHE SWEET / IF YOU LOVE ME, BABY

UK Release: Polydor NH 52-317, 29 May 1964 (SP)
Recording data: 22 June 1961 at Friedrich-Ebert-Halle and Studio Rahlstedt, Hamburg, Germany
Producer: Bert Kaempfert
Engineer: Karl Hinze

At the height of Beatlemania, *Polydor* seized upon releasing this single – taken from their first Hamburg recording session – because it featured Lennon on lead vocals. It reached number 29 in the UK chart.

This version (which has Pete Best on drums) was later included on the *Anthology 1* album, while a recording from the sessions for *Abbey Road* (with Starr, natch) was released on *Anthology 3* – making it the only song to appear on two of the *Anthology* albums. Furthermore, a solo Lennon rendering, taped during his 'lost weekend' phase, was included in the *John Lennon Anthology* box set in 1998. As it was a featured part of the band's early repertoire – inspired by the track on Gene Vincent's *Bluejean Baby* album, when the band were still The Quarrymen – it was clearly a song that the lads had a lot of affection for. Unlike 'My Bonnie'.

On this release, the b-side (also known as 'Take Out Some Insurance On Me, Baby') was credited to "The Beatles with Tony Sheridan, vocal".

NEW DISC SIGNINGS

Former Beatle's debut on Decca

PETE BEST, former drummer with the Beatles, makes his debut on the Decca label on June 19 with his own group, the Pete Best Four. Titles are "I'm Gonna Knock On Your Door" and "Why Did I Fall In Love With You."

Best is likely to sign an agency contract with the Grade Organisation shortly.

THE FIRST VOCAL DISC BY JOHN LENNON

polydor WITH **THE BEATLES**

AIN'T SHE SWEET

AVAILABLE NOW ON POLYDOR 52 317 (single)

MONTH-LONG HOLIDAY FOR BEATLES

THE Beatles begin a 4-week "secret holiday" this weekend. The group has no further commitments until its appearance at the Prince of Wales theatre on May 31.

"The boys are resting after completing their film. Their plans for the rest of the month are very confidential," Brian Epstein told the NME on Wednesday.

Next Wednesday they will, of course, be seen in the Rediffusion-TV spectacular "Around The Beatles" which they completed filming on Tuesday. The hour-long show features several other artists including Cilla Black and Millie.

The Beatles are spotlighted in two editions of Radio Luxembourg's "This Is Their Life" series on May 10 and 17.

During a Press Reception after their arrival in Edinburgh on Wednesday, the Beatles were asked for £100,000 by the Lord Provost, Duncan Weatherstone, towards the Edinburgh International Festival.

"I am not joking," he said. "I thought they might like to help other aspects of music and art." John Lennon countered: "It was a good try but we haven't got any loose change."

Paul added: "We hear he tries this with everybody!"

Brian Epstein reveals plans for . . .

BEATLES' XMAS SHOW

NEW EP, 'LUCKY STARS' DATE, AND RADIO SHOW

THE BEATLES will star in another glittering Christmas show this year. It will be staged at the Rank Organisation's largest theatre, Hammersmith Odeon, Brian Epstein revealed to the NME this week. Other Beatles news: a new EP is being issued in a fortnight; the group has been booked for another "Thank Your Lucky Stars" appearance and a major radio date.

The Beatles' Yuletide show will open at Hammersmith Odeon on Christmas Eve and run twice-nightly at the theatre—which seats nearly 3,500 people—until January 16. It will be presented by Brian Epstein in association with Joe Collins and produced by Peter Yolland who was responsible for their last Christmas show—at Finsbury Park Astoria.

As in the previous production, the Beatles will be seen throughout the show. Other well-known stars are being sought to join them. Sounds Incorporated are already set.

There is a possibility that the show may play some Northern dates after its London run.

Bookings for the show cannot be accepted until the box office opens at the end of the summer.

"LONG TALL SALLY" EP

After tremendous demand, EMI has decided to issue a Beatles EP featuring Paul McCartney's version of "Long Tall Sally" on June 19. Also included will be Ringo's version of the Carl Perkins number "Matchbox," the Lennon-McCartney composition "I Call Your Name" and "Slow Down."

The Beatles return to ABC-TV's "Thank Your Lucky Stars" on July 11. It will be their first appearance on the show since the all-Liverpool edition last December.

The Beatles are to star in the first of the Light Programme's new Thursday night pop shows on July 16 (10-11.55 pm). The series will—as revealed last week—be introduced by Brian Matthew and produced by Bernie Andrews.

The Beatles film "A Hard Day's Night" will now have an American premiere—in New York on August 12—although John, Paul, George and Ringo will not be able to attend.

● Screening of ATV's documentary "The Road To Beatlemania" has been put back a week to Wednesday, July 15.

New Beatle—but only till Sunday

RINGO STARR will rejoin the Beatles at London Airport on Sunday morning after being the first member of the group to be replaced since it came to fame.

Jimmy Nichols, 24-year-old drummer with Georgie Fame's Blue Flames, was flying to Copenhagen with John, Paul and George yesterday (Thursday) to deputise for Ringo who was admitted to the University College Hospital in London on Wednesday after being taken ill suddenly with laryngitis.

But the other Beatles expect Ringo to be waiting for them when they fly into London Airport from Amsterdam on Sunday morning on their way to Australia for their first tour "down under."

Although Wednesday was set aside for recording, Ringo's illness will not delay release of the Beatles' next single—due out early next month. Tracks had been completed and the Wednesday sessions were scheduled for vocal dual-tracking only.

Recording at the BBC
© David Magnus / Rex

LONG TALL SALLY

UK Release: Parlophone GEP-8913, 19 June 1964 (EP)
Recording data: 1 March and 1 June 1964, EMI Studios, London
Producer: George Martin
Engineer: Norman Smith
Tracks: Long Tall Sally / I Call Your Name / Slow Down / Matchbox

---

"One of the things I didn't like about the film Backbeat is that they gave 'Long Tall Sally' to the John character. I was not amused. I always sang that: me and Little Richard."
– Paul McCartney

The first genuinely worthwhile extended play, with all 'new' material, has sleeve notes written by Derek Taylor, who would be the Beatles press officer on and off for the rest of his life. He was taken on by Epstein for their first US tour, doubling as the manager's personal assistant and the band's PR man. But Epstein quickly became envious of his close friendship with his boys, and their relationship became very strained. Taylor quit his dual role as soon as the tour ended, saying, "I'm not taking any more of this man's shit. I love the Beatles but I'm not hanging around to be fired another hundred times." After Epstein passed away, he returned to become *Apple's* press officer.

In his notes, Taylor alludes to the public's craving for more product, and this could certainly be seen as a bit of a stop-gap, containing as it does three rock and roll classics from the band's early repertoire (though a three month break between new releases is nothing by today's standards). But as soon as you hear McCartney belting out the lyrics to Little Richard's best-seller, then Harrison's cracking solo, you know this is no band treading water.

Obviously Taylor's claim that the band had enough of their own material "to keep them busy for the next ten years," was phooey, but they were smart enough to include one of their compositions to help boost royalties.

Lennon wrote 'I Call Your Name' when the band were still in Liverpool, but "added the middle eight when we came down to London". He had first bequeathed the piece to Billy J. Kramer, whose version was released on the b-side of his single 'Bad To Me' – another song from the Lennon and McCartney canon.

They recorded 'I Call Your Name' in the same three hour session that produced 'Long Tall Sally' and 'I'm Happy Just To Dance With You'. It was intended that the song would appear in their first feature film, but director Richard Lester knocked that idea on the head. Too much cowbell, perhaps? There would be plenty of that in the title song, already. This song also featured Harrison playing his *Rickenbacker 360* 12-string, about which he told *Melody Maker*, "It's gear. It sounds a bit like an electric piano... you get a nice fat sound out of it."

This EP was released on the day JFK's youngest brother, Senator Edward Kennedy, was seriously injured in a private plane crash that killed the pilot, in Massachusetts.

A HARD DAY'S NIGHT / THINGS WE SAID TODAY

UK Release: Parlophone R 5160, 10 July 1964 (SP)
Recording data: 16 April & 2 June 1964, EMI Studios, London.
Producer: George Martin
Engineer: Norman Smith

"Dick Lester said we are going to use that title, and the next morning I brought in the song. 'Cause there was a little competition between Paul and I as to who got the A side, who got the hit singles." **– John Lennon**

This was the band's first single to break away from the ruse of putting I, Me or You in the title ("so it was very direct and personal", was how McCartney had put it) and instead went with an off-the-cuff remark made by Starr about the group's heavy workload. The song is featured prominently throughout the film of the same name, which premiered in the UK just four days earlier.

After it was agreed that *A Hard Day's Night* would be the title of the already near-completed film, Lennon quickly tossed this off, wanting to beat McCartney to the punch. The song has recorded just as quickly a few days later, with Lennon leaving the high notes to his credited co-composer. Lennon was in fact on a bit of a roll at this time, coming up with the bulk of the songs on the soundtrack album thus asserting his perceived authority over the band.

Now used to utilising the four-track recording techniques, the basic backing track for the song was put together first, before adding vocals and, finally, overdubbing the distinctive piano/guitar solo duet by the two Georges.

"We wanted a particularly strong and effective beginning," said Martin, and starting with a single "strident guitar" chord (an Fadd9, according to Harrison) was indeed an original and striking way of kicking off the film/single/album. Altogether, something of a mini masterpiece.

On the b-side, 'Things We Said Today' goes from ballad to rock and back again in a way the band - and many thousands of bands since - would repeatedly do. This worked particularly well in a live environment, as evidenced by the version on *The Beatles At The Hollywood Bowl* album.

On release, the single and the *A Hard Day's Night* soundtrack album went straight to the toppermost; it was the first time anyone held the top spots simultaneously in both charts on either side of the North Atlantic. The song won a Grammy for best performance by a vocal group the following year.

A HARD DAY'S NIGHT

UK Release: Parlophone PMC 1230 (mono) / PCS 3058 (stereo), 19 July 1964 (LP)
US Release: United Artists UAL-3366, 26 June 1964 (LP)
Recording data: 29 January, 25–27 February, 1 March & 1–4 June 1964, EMI Studios, London, and Pathé Marconi Studios, Paris
Producer: George Martin
Engineer: Norman Smith
Tracks: A Hard Day's Night / I Should Have Known Better / If I Fell / I'm Happy Just To Dance With You / And I Love Her / Tell Me Why / Can't Buy Me Love / Any Time At All / I'll Cry Instead / Things We Said Today / When I Get Home / You Can't Do That / I'll Be Back

---

"If you look at our itinerary some of those years where we did maybe a tour of England, a tour of Europe, a tour of America, two albums and about four EPs and three singles and made a movie all in the same year you think Jesus, how did we do that?" – **George Harrison**

1964 was one such incredibly busy year for the Fabs, with concerts all over - from Scarborough to Hong Kong – and their first full tour of North America. Lennon also had his first book of nonsense verse and doodles published (*In His Own Write*), and the band made their first feature film, *A Hard Day's Night*.

The songs for the accompanying soundtrack album were accordingly hastily written by the dynamic duo. Whilst the songs might not have covered any new ground or musically made any significant progress (save perhaps for Harrson's extensive use of his *Rickenbacker* 12-string guitar, first heard on the *Long Tall Sally* E.P.), it's nigh on impossible to find fault with anything on offer here.

Of course, it's conceivable that the Beatles bubble might've burst after the first couple of years, so this album was really crucial in ensuring their continued success. And they really showed they had some balls here.

This was their first album of all original material, the first recorded completely on four-track tape, and the only one credited solely to Lennon & McCartney (though the former came up with the bulk of these new songs).

'I'll Cry Instead' was intended to appear in the *A Hard Day's Night* film, but director Lester apparently didn't like that song either and it was cut at the last minute. The song did though appear on the US version of the *A Hard Day's Night* original soundtrack album (released ahead of its UK counterpart), alongside the seven songs performed by the Beatles in the film plus four Martin-arranged easy listening orchestral versions of 'I Should Have Known Better', 'And I Love Her', Ringo's Theme ('This Boy') and 'A Hard Day's Night'.

'I Should Have Known Better' reveals Lennon's emerging infatuation with Bob Dylan and his final use of the harmonica during the intro of a Beatles song.

Following the first two up-tempo numbers, 'If I Fell' (a third consecutive song predominantly from the pen of Lennon) slows the pace a tad and has a two-part harmony sung by Lennon and McCartney into a single microphone – in the style of the Everlys. The young me was very puzzled by the "when she learns we are two" line, as I thought they sang "she-lands", which makes no sense – hence the confusion. As mondegreens go, it's pretty crap, but I still sing it that way.

On this album, Starr had no solo spot, but Harrison got to sing 'I'm Happy Just To Dance With You', which Lennon wrote specifically for him. McCartney also subsequently credited Harrison with coming up with the guitar riff on 'And I Love Her' – which he rightly says is the song. Indeed, despite what some say about the 'the quiet one', both

Lennon and McCartney always encouraged him to be more visible and involved.

Of 'Tell Me Why', McCartney was later to say that it was likely "based in real experiences or affairs John was having, or arguments with Cynthia", something Lennon himself would openly admit with the following year's 'Norwegian Wood'. But at the time, it was just a great "shuffle number that comes at the end of the film" (in Lennon's words). Lennon dismissed 'Any Time At All' as an attempt at rewriting 'It Won't Be Long'. The song was recorded during the last sessions for the album and remained incomplete: the brief instrumental section towards the end was supposed to be decorated with more lyrics, but they simply ran out of time.

'When I Get Home' and 'I'll Be Back' are further Lennon-led compositions, the latter being directly inspired by the chords to Del Shannon's 'Runaway'. It fades away rather unexpectedly and ends the band's shortest album, clocking it in at just over half an hour.

The album was released less than a month before the last ever executions took place in the United Kingdom – one of them in Walton Prison, Liverpool – prior to capital punishment finally being abolished (in all circumstances) in 1998.

SOMETHING NEW

US Release: Capitol ST-2108, 10 April 1964 (LP)

Recording data: 29 January, 25–27 February, 1 March &1–4 June 1964, Pathé Marconi Studios, Paris & EMI Studios, London

Producer: George Martin

Engineer: Norman Smith

Tracks: I'll Cry Instead / Things We Said Today / Any Time At All / When I Get Home / Slow Down / Matchbox / Tell Me Why / And I Love Her / I'm Happy Just To Dance With You / If I Fell / Komm, Gib Mir Deine Hand

---

Another compilation of material – some 'new' to the North American market - based around tracks from the UK's *A Hard Day's Night* album. Some of the mixes differ, and some of the tracks appeared on the US version of *A Hard Day's Night*. In parlance of our times, "WTF?"

Beatle George nearly nearly cut to ribbons !

YES, the Beatles are home and well after the longest holiday of their working lives. We've seen the pictures of their carefree smiles and suntanned faces. But the best kept secret of the whole trip involves an incident that almost cost the Beatles George Harrison !

He explained to me on Sunday: "John and I took up all sorts of weird sports that we had always wanted to try our hand at while we were in the Caribbean.

"Anyway, this particular day we went water ski-ing. I was going along quite happily towards the shore and the boatman made a normal turn out towards the open ocean—but he'd left it a bit too late and before I'd realised what was happening, I was skimming over the top of razor-sharp coral, which was almost on the surface.

"I dread to think what would have happened if the water had been an inch shallower. I would have been cut to ribbons ! I can tell you it was about the nastiest moment of my life."

As it is, George will bear a scar from his holiday for a long time to come. After harpooning a fish which had a razor-edged fin, he threw it towards the shore. The fin cut across his hand and gashed into his thumb deeply.

"This one hurt, I can tell you," he said, showing me a deep scar on the inside of his thumb.

Angry

Despite the publicity their trips attracted, the Beatles were unhampered by reporters for much of the time.

"Brian Epstein expected us to come back all angry because we hadn't had any peace. But it was quite the opposite," explained John. "We had a ball !"

This was partly due, I suspect, to their frequent changes of plan throughout the holiday.

"We went out via Honolulu and intended to come back that way, but changed our minds at the last moment. We looked in on Las Vegas on the return journey," George told me.

"It's a fab city and although we were only there four hours, we probably saw more of it than we will when we go back officially in August ! The airline people laid on a car and drove us all around the famous spots," he added.

Despite the month's separation of songwriters Lennon and McCartney, several new Beatles hits are likely to emerge from the holiday. For while they were resting in the sun, John penned five new numbers and Paul made a good start on two. George put pen to paper as well and came up with two songs.

Ringo

Soon after returning to London Ringo began making plans to send his parents to Scotland for a holiday. Though George Harrison sent his mum and dad to Montego Bay, Ringo isn't trying to save money.

"My dad doesn't like flying so it is much better that they should have a holiday in Britain," Ringo told me.

John Lennon's Aunt Mimi will spend her vacation in Australia—she leaves with the boys on Sunday for their trip "down under" as part of a special treat that all four Beatles helped to plan.

The Beatles spent most of Monday, Tuesday and Wednesday afternoons and evenings in the recording studios waxing their next single—a non-film title which will be issued early next month.

THEY HAD TO REHEARSE !

THEY'VE been away so long that the Beatles had to REHEARSE their performance for Brian Epstein's concerts at London's Prince of Wales theatre on Sunday. But the holiday did them good—though its content remained pretty much the same their act was refreshed and all four were obviously pleased to be working again.

It was also refreshing to see the Prince of Wales full on a Sunday night. Fans filled the seats and overspilled to standing positions all around the theatre to watch George, John, Paul and Ringo hammer their way through favourites like "Can't Buy Me Love," "All My Loving" and soften up for "This Boy."

George pleased his admirers with "Roll Over Beethoven" and Paul his with "Till There Was You." They finished another sensational Beatles' performance with what now seems to be their dual show-stoppers—"Twist And Shout," followed by "Long Tall Sally."

Maybe it was the sheer vitality of the Beatles that inspired other acts on the bill to all give plus performances. Particularly impressive was Laurie Jay's new combo with some funny impressions of the Bachelors, Freddie and the Dreamers, and others.

EXTRACTS FROM THE FILM A HARD DAY'S NIGHT

UK Release: Parlophone GEP 8920, 4 November 1964 (EP)
Recording data: 1964, EMI Studios, London
Producer: George Martin
Engineer: Norman Smith
Tracks: I Should Have Known Better / If I Fell / Tell Me Why / And I Love Her

---

I guess I should have known better, but I was one of the suckers who fell for this and helped this collection of four songs from the soundtrack album reach the number one spot in the UK. I can only guess that I couldn't yet afford to buy the full album.

Ludwig
THE
BEATLES

EXTRACTS FROM THE FILM A HARD DAY'S NIGHT

UK Release: Parlophone GEP 8924, 6 November 1964 (EP)
Recording data: 1964, EMI Studios, London
Producer: George Martin
Engineer: Norman Smith
Tracks: Any Time at All / I'll Cry Instead / Things We Said Today / When I Get Home

---

Oh no, not a second time!

A second batch of excerpts from the soundtrack album, released just two days after the first. This merely begs the question: why did they not include either 'I'm Happy Just To Dance With You' or 'I'll Be Back', instead of 'Things We Said Today'; that would then have left just one track unreleased on a 7 inch platter in the UK.

Makes no sense. Maybe that's why it only reached number eight in the hit parade? I didn't get this one.

THE BEATLES' STORY

US Release: Capitol STBO-2222, 23 November 1964 (LP)
Recording data: Capitol Records Building and The Hollywood Bowl, Hollywood, California
Producer: John Babcock, Roger Christian, and Al Wiman (documentary); George Martin (music).
Tracks: On Stage With The Beatles / How Beatlemania Began / Beatlemania In Action / Man Behind The Beatles — Brian Epstein / John Lennon / Who's A Millionaire? / Beatles Will Be Beatles / Man Behind The Music — George Martin / George Harrison / A Hard Day's Night — Their First Movie / Paul McCartney / Sneaky Haircuts And More About Paul / The Beatles Look At Life / Victims' Of Beatlemania / Beatle Medley / Ringo Starr / Liverpool And All The World!

An assemblage of interviews and press conferences that also included stereo snippets from their 1964 Hollywood Bowl concert. This documentary double album was *Capitol's* fifth release, and uses a questionable apostrophe in its title.

I FEEL FINE / SHE'S A WOMAN

UK Release: Parlophone R 5200, 27 November 1964 (SP)
US Release: Capitol 5327, 23 November 1964 (SP)
Recording data: 8 and 18 October 1964, EMI Studios, London
Producer: George Martin
Engineer: Norman Smith

"I wrote this at a recording session. It was tied together around the guitar riff that opens it." **– John Lennon**

'I Feel Fine' is the first ever studio recording – by anyone, anywhere – that intentionally included feedback. Said McCartney "John had a semi-acoustic *Gibson* guitar. It had a pickup on it so it could be amplified... we were just about to walk away to listen to a take when John leaned his guitar against the amp. I can still see him doing it... it went, 'Nnnnnnwahhhhh!' And we went, 'What's that? Voodoo!' 'No, it's feedback.' ' Wow, it's a great sound!' George Martin was there so we said, 'Can we have that on the record?' 'Well, I suppose we could, we could edit it on the front.'"

Written immediately after recording 'Eight Days A Week' for the band's next album, Lennon initially dismissed 'I Feel Fine' as "lousy", but recognised its potential once the band started to play it.

The guitar riff was influenced by a record called 'Watch Your Step' by Bobby Parker, one of Lennon's favourite records. Its double-tracked sound was simply Lennon and Harrison playing the same line.

When this was performed by the Fabs on TV, I came running in from the garden with my brother to see Lennon pretend he had an electric razor and shaved his chinny-chin-chin during the intro. My how we laughed. Brother Steve had fashioned himself a *Höfner* violin bass like McCartney's from some old bits of wood, with the strings pencilled on, and played along.

'She's A Woman' was a real belter from McCartney, striving to capture the spirit of Little Richard. Like most of their b-sides, it was certainly no throwaway, and was regularly featured in their live set.

BEATLES FOR SALE

UK Release: Parlophone PMC 1240 (mono) / PCS 3062 (stereo), 4 December 1964 (LP)
Recording data: 11–14 August, 29 September & 26 October 1964, EMI Studios, London
Producer: George Martin
Engineer: Norman Smith
Tracks: No Reply / I'm A Loser / Baby's In Black / Rock And Roll Music / I'll Follow The Sun / Mr. Moonlight / Medley: Kansas City-Hey, Hey, Hey, Hey! / Eight Days A Week / Words Of Love / Honey Don't / Every Little Thing / I Don't Want To Spoil The Party / What You're Doing / Everybody's Trying To Be My Baby

---

"The rehearsal would go on in the studio because from very early on a lot of the songs weren't finished, the ideas were there for the songs or the first verse or a chorus but it could be changed by the writers as we were doing it." – **Ringo Starr**

Unnecessarily rushed and arguably their weakest album. Actually, no – it is their poorest effort. *Beatles For Sale*, like the *Long Tall Sally* EP before it, features a bevy of rock and roll standards alongside a few impressive originals, such as Lennon's 'I'm A Loser'.

Lennon would later declare, "Part of me suspects I'm a loser, and part of me thinks I'm God Almighty!" and, quite understandably, all of the band must by now have been feeling like Supermen with all the adulation they were receiving. On their trips to America they were being introduced to the likes of Bob Dylan, Cassius Clay (shortly before he beat Sonny Liston to become the world heavyweight boxing champion and converted to the Nation of Islam to become Muhammad Ali), and a whole array of film stars – many of them demanding to see the boys. As a result, they felt able to speak their minds and, perhaps unwittingly, made some pretty bold statements. In September 1964, for instance, the States was far from united and the band was expected to play to a racially segregated audience in Jacksonville, Florida. But they refused, deeming the very notion "daft". Kudos, lads!

So it is therefore a shame that they let themselves be pushed into making what is overall a below par album – but one which nevertheless sold by the truckload. And although I don't rate it as one of the great Beatles' albums, it is still superior to many other albums I could name. It may just show a hint of uncertainty in a young band about to really find their feet and venturing off into more mature pastures.

Lyrically, the first three tracks set the glum tone of the record: 'No Reply' is about being blanked by a deceitful girlfriend; 'I'm A Loser' describes the reality behind Lennon's brave face (in his rather stuffy but informative memoir, John, Paul, George, Ringo & Me, press officer Tony Barrow confirms the insecure and sensitive soul behind the bold exterior); and 'Baby's In Black' is Macca's paean to Sutcliffe's grieving girlfriend, Astrid Kirchherr.

After the upbeat spirit and derring-do of the previous album, this all sounds rather morose in comparison. And the album's title may give an insight into how they were feeling in the full-on glare of Beatlemania. One look at their faces on the cover says it all. And even some of the cover songs are a tad suspect: 'Mr. Moonlight', I'm looking at you. Although the band had included this Dr. Feelgood And The Interns b-side in their live act for a couple of years, its obscurity didn't actually equate to being any good. They had also been playing the similar (at least, in my eyes) 'Bésame Mucho' live for a while longer, but thankfully didn't think to record and release a version during the lifetime of the band (despite clearly having a lot of fun messing around with it during the filming of the *Let It Be* movie). Yes, they could do so much better with Latin percussion and a *Hammond* organ.

But there is still much to be admired about this album. 'I'll Follow The Sun' is an old pre-Beatles McCartney song that the band had shied away from recording before. Although they had already shown a softer side with songs like 'This Boy', 'And I Love Her' and 'If I Fell', 'I'll Follow The Sun' had previously been considered a bit too far away from their tough rock 'n' roll image. But at this point in time they were trying hard not to repeat the formula and decided to give this melancholy ballad a chance. And as it happens, this is definitely one of the best songs on the album.

'Eight Days A Week' is another song, like 'All My Loving', that people just know and could so easily have been released as a top-selling single in this country, but wasn't. It also displays a hint of the experimentation that was to come, with the song being faded in instead of out

And lyrically, Lennon was now beginning to write more personal lyrics (albeit still about luvnstuf), like those for 'I Don't Want To Spoil The Party', in which an agitated and uncertain Lennon is stood up by some gal so leaves the party rather bringing everyone else down.

'What You're Doing' could be seen as a foretaste of the sound the Byrds would soon claim as their own, with lyrics expressing doubt about McCartney's relationship with Asher.

The album ends in a less sombre mood than it started with a cover of Carl Perkins' boastful 'Everybody's Trying to Be My Baby'. American rockabilly musician Perkins, who recorded at the legendary Sun Records Studio in Memphis in the mid-50s and wrote 'Blue Suede Shoes', also penned 'Honey Don't', which Starr sings on this album. But Harrison (who was a huge fan of Perkins' and would attend his funeral in 1998) takes the lead here, with loads of echo applied to his vocals. The song has a false ending, something the band had developed during live performances in the past.

As I say, not a bad album – just not a great Beatles' one!

ANOTHER BEATLES CHRISTMAS RECORD

UK Release: Lyntone LYN 757, 26 October 1964 (SP)
Recording data: 18 December 1964, Dick James Music, London
Producer: Tony Barrow

At some point in the early eighties, I wandered into a second-hand shop in Bromley and stumbled upon this record. Amazed at my discovery, I nervously asked the store-keep how much he wanted for it. "35...?" he said. "How much?!" I exclaimed. "Oh, alright – 25...p," he countered. While it was not in mint condition, it's perfectly playable and it's worth considerably more than I paid for it. No doubt. Barg'in!

Another largely spoken word recording helmed by the hapless Barrow, whose script is muchly enhanced by the zany foursome... it says here.

THE EARLY BEATLES

US Release: Capitol ST-2309, 22 March 1965 (LP)
Recording data: 4 & 11 September, 26 & 30 November 1962; 11, 20 & 25 February 1963, EMI Studios, London
Producer: George Martin
Engineer: Norman Smith
Tracks: Love Me Do / Twist and Shout / Anna (Go to Him) / Chains / Boys / Ask Me Why / Please Please Me / P.S. I Love You / Baby It's You / A Taste of Honey / Do You Want to Know a Secret

---

While most of *Capitol's* album releases were collections of material first released in the band's home country during the preceding 12 months (give or take), *The Early Beatles* came out two years after the *Please Please Me* album, from whence all of its tracks are taken. It also finally put paid to the album released by *Vee-Jay*, whose license to distribute the band's recordings expired in October 1964.

BEATLES FOR SALE

UK Release: Parlophone GEP 8931, 6 April 1965 (EP)
Recording data: 1965, EMI Studios, London
Producer: George Martin
Engineer: Norman Smith
Tracks: No Reply / I'm a Loser / Rock And Roll Music / Eight Days A Week

---

Released only in mono, this was the group's eighth official EP. It sold well. It sat at the top of the EP charts for a total of six weeks.

TICKET TO RIDE / YES IT IS

UK Release: Parlophone R 5265, 9 April 1965 (SP)
US Release: Capitol 5407, 19 April 1965 (SP)
Recording data: 15-16 February 1965, EMI Studios, London
Producer: George Martin
Engineer: Norman Smith

"That was one of the earliest heavy-metal records made. Paul's contribution was the way Ringo played the drums." – **John Lennon**

1965 was an incredibly busy year for the Fabs... yes, I know I said that about 1964 too, but listen to this: Starr married Maureen Cox and they had their first child together (Zak); Lennon passed his driving test and published his second book (*A Spaniard In The Works*); McCartney and Starr bought houses, in St John's Wood and Weybridge respectively; they toured Europe; completed a second full US tour – including their record-breaking first performance at New York's Shea Stadium, watched by 55,600 fans; they toured the UK for the last time; they made their second feature film (*Help!*); made numerous appearances on radio and TV, including a fourth Ed Sullivan Show; they became Members of the Most Excellent Order of the British Empire; it was the last time they recorded and released two full albums in one year (and what a couple of corkers they were!); they finally got to meet the idol of their youths (Elvis Presley – though that turned out to be a little disappointing, with Lennon commenting that Engelbert Humperdinck had been more fun); and they took LSD for the first time.

Anyhow, this was their first new release of the year and, interestingly, the composers offered very different accounts of the song's meaning, which probably reveal more about the pair of them than the song itself. McCartney said it referred simply to having a rail ticket to go to Ryde – a seaside town on the Isle Of Wight; Lennon though insisted it was a reference back to Hamburg days when prostitutes were given a card by their doctors to say they were clean. Very clean.

'Ticket To Ride' was the first song by the band on which McCartney played lead guitar. And U2 later half-inched part of the drum pattern (which as noted above, was suggested by McCartney) for their 'Sunday Bloody Sunday'. Maybe someday Charles Manson will steal it back?

'Yes It Is' remains to this day one of my all time favourite Beatles' songs of all time. The seemingly effortless three-part harmony vocals and Harrison's special guitar effects make it all just so... transplendent.

BEATLES FOR SALE (No. 2)

UK Release: Parlophone GEP 8938, 4 June 1965 (EP)
Recording data: 1965, EMI Studios, London
Producer: George Martin
Engineer: Norman Smith
Tracks: I'll Follow The Sun / Baby's In Black / Words Of Love / I Don't Want To Spoil The Party

---

Released in mono only, another four tracks from the last album. It had a nice colour photograph of the boys on the front cover.

BEATLES VI

US Release: Capitol ST-2358, 14 June 1965 (LP)
Recording data: 29–30 September, 6–18 & 26 October 1964, 16–18 February & 10 May 1965, EMI Studios, London
Producer: George Martin
Engineer: Norman Smith
Tracks: Medley: Kansas City-Hey, Hey, Hey, Hey! / Eight Days A Week / You Like Me Too Much / Bad Boy / I Don't Want To Spoil The Party / Words Of Love / What You're Doing / Yes It Is / Dizzy Miss Lizzie (sic) / Tell Me What You See / Every Little Thing

---

The title here takes into account the 'compilations' *The Beatles' Story* and *The Early Beatles*, ignores *United Artists' A Hard Day's Night*, and tramps the dirt down on the *Vee-Jay* album.

HELP! / I'M DOWN

UK Release: Parlophone R 5305, 23 July 1965 (SP)
US Release: Capitol 5476, 19 July 1965 (SP)
Recording data: 13 April & 14 June 1965, EMI Studios, London
Producer: George Martin
Engineer: Norman Smith

"I seem to remember sitting around and thinking, What are we going to call this one? Somehow Help! came out. John went home and thought about it and got the basis of it, then we had a writing session on it. I would have to credit it to John for original inspiration 70-30. My main contribution is the countermelody to John." – **Paul McCartney**

Although Lennon claimed 'Help!' as one of his most honest songs for the Beatles, one that wasn't 'written to order', it was only composed after an agreement had been reached about the title of the film they had very nearly completed. I guess we should be thankful that they didn't go with the film's working title of 'Eight Arms To Hold You'. Can you imagine?

It was with the benefit of hindsight that anyone actually saw this as the cry for, er, help that it was from a bloated and depressed Lennon. Even he claimed not to have realised it at the time. Although he was the song's main composer, McCartney has stated that Lennon needed a kick up the arse else the song may never have gotten finished. And so it was it got finished. The song starts with no musical intro – everything (voice/drums/guitars) chiming in all at once, a trick they almost repeated with 'We Can Work It Out' six months later.

Like 'Please Please Me', the song was conceived as a slow paced ballad, but the boys were again encouraged to ratchet things up a gnat's and make it a fast rock 'n' roll number. Just to please please the masses, you understand. This was something Lennon later regretted, but in my capacity as a representative of the masses, I found it to be yet another most agreeable beat record. Definitely not their finest single by any means, but pretty darn memorable – not least because it opens one of my all time favourite films (one which remains in my top ten to this day – copies of the complete list are available on request).

And the b-side elevates the release muchly in mine eyes. A McCartney song that would quickly replace 'Long Tall Sally' as a set closer on the band's final tours - something he probably hoped to achieve, as 'I'm Down' is very much in the vein of little Richard Penniman's oeuvre. Lyrically a little downbeat, like its a-side, but a big bunch more tongue in cheek. The recording features Lennon on organ, a role he would famously reprise during the band's gig at Shea Stadium a month after its release.

HELP!

UK Release: Parlophone PMC 1255 (mono) / PCS 3071 (stereo), 6 August 1965 (LP)
US Release: Capitol MAS-2386 (mono) / SMAS-2386 (stereo), 13 August 1965 (LP)
Recording data: 15–19 February, 13 April, 10 May & 14–17 June 1965, EMI Studios, London
Producer: George Martin
Engineer: Norman Smith
Tracks: Help! / The Night Before / You've Got to Hide Your Love Away / I Need You / Another Girl / You're Going to Lose That Girl / Ticket to Ride / Act Naturally / It's Only Love / You Like Me Too Much / Tell Me What You See / I've Just Seen a Face / Yesterday / Dizzy Miss Lizzy

---

"I had these two guys who used to write songs whenever we needed some. I think we just called them up and said, Look we'll be doing a movie now lads, will you come up with a couple of catchy hits?!" – **George Harrison**

Yes, Harrison himself did indeed come up with two songs here that were the equal of his big brothers' efforts. And the one that was written for the film but which got relegated to the b-side ('You Like Me Too Much') is arguably the better, with its composer's double-tracked lead vocals and Lennon's subtle *Hohner* Pianet electric piano accompaniment. Oh yes.

The other, his second song ever to be recorded by the band, was 'I Need You'. Written for his wife Pattie, it made the film and employed some untypical percussion ideas: Starr battered the back of a Gibson Jumbo acoustic guitar, while Lennon played a snare drum throughout. Wacky.

There are some who write off both *Help!* the film and *Help!* the album as inferior to *A Hard Day's Night*. Don't listen to them: they've clearly been taken in by a drug-addled Lennon in his gnarly post-Beatles period. The film has far more of a story - it isn't centred around the band's everyday life, and it sees them showing off their Marx Bros/Goon Show influenced humour in glorious living Technicolor in exotic locations around the globe (thanks to the bigger bucks the success of the previous low-budget black and white movie inevitably lead to).

Hell, fantasy beats mundane reality every time, doesn't it? And the album goes from pop/rock to bluegrass, folk to classical, and even puts the cunt in country and western - their most varied collection thus far, no question. A real move away from the Mersey beat sound.

Yep, I personally prefer *Help!* – motion picture and long player. But that's not to say *A Hard Day's Night* doesn't run them a very close second. There is no question that they ever made a better film after this one, though had they agreed to film Joe Orton's Up Against It, they just maybe might've.

English playwright Orton was asked to submit a screenplay for the follow-up to *Help!* in 1967. The script would have seen the boys dress in drag, deflower a priest's niece, and consort with anarchists to assassinate the Prime Minister. It ends with them all marrying the same girl and it is thus not very hard to fathom why the script was later returned with no comment. Not long after, in August 1967, Orton would be bludgeoned to death with a hammer by his lover Kenneth Halliwell, who then committed suicide. At Orton's funeral, a tape of the Beatles' 'A Day In The Life' was played.

Anyway, back to *Help!*, which pretty much lit the blue touch-paper to the band's gobsmacking musical creativity about to follow.

Keeping the personal recollections going for a minute, this was the first album my big brother ever owned; my parents bought it for his 12th birthday, and scribbled their best wishes on the back sleeve. Some years later, the shiny film on the front cover started to peel off.

The front cover of course famously shows the boys spelling out the word OUCH in semaphore.

Okay, it's doesn't actually say that. It should have read HELP, but photographer Freeman said, "the arrangement of the arms with those letters didn't look good. So we decided to improvise and ended up with the best graphic positioning of the arms." So while totally meaningless, NUJV was more aesthetically pleasing – as well as being educational: I'd never heard of artistic license before then.

If you don't count the brief inclusion of a tongue-in-cheek version of a traditional Liverpool folk song on their final album, *Help!* is the last time the band recorded any cover tunes, viz Buck Owens and the Buckaroos' country number one 'Act Naturally' and Larry Williams' 'Dizzy Miss Lizzy'.

Lennon and McCartney's 'If You've Got Trouble' was intended to be Ringo's customary one lead vocal contribution, but the band were unhappy with the recording and opted for 'Act Naturally' instead. 'If You've Got Trouble' is nothing like as memorable. While Starr's drumming on 'Tell Me What You See' appears to echo parts of his playing on 'Ticket To Ride', you should check out his overdubbed bongo fury on 'You're Going To Lose That Girl'. Hotcha!

'You've Got To Hide Your Love Away' was the first Beatles song to feature an 'outsider': flautist Johnnie Scott. And what a song it is! Lennon always cited Bob Dylan as influencing these lyrics, which were an expression of his emotions rather than some imagined situation. It also signals a move towards greater use of acoustic instrumentation.

As per *A Hard Day's Night*, the *Help!* album featured one side of music from the fillum of the same name, and then a bunch of filler on the b-side. So neither is strictly a soundtrack album.

I say 'filler' in jest, obviously: 'Yesterday' is today one of the most covered songs in the history of recorded music, with well over 2,000 renditions roaming the planet. For such a hugely successful song, it is noteworthy for the fact that McCartney is the only actual Beatle to appear on this recording and that its use of session musicians shewed an open-mindedness and willingness by the band to expand their horizons.

The song had been brewing in McCartney's nogging for some while before being finally completed. Said Lennon, "Every time we got together to write songs, this one would come up. Paul wrote nearly all of it, but we just couldn't find the right title. We called it 'Scrambled Eggs' and it became a joke between us. We made up our minds that only a one-word title would suit. Then one morning Paul woke up and the song and the title were both there, completed. I was sorry in a way, we'd had so many laughs about it." The album was released five days before the Watts riots started in downtown LA, which resulted in 34 deaths, over 1000 injuries and Frank Zappa's 'Trouble Every Day'. Yes, the times they were a-changing.

WE CAN WORK IT OUT / DAY TRIPPER

UK Release: Parlophone R 5389, 3 December 1965 (SP)
US Release: Capitol 5555, 3 December 1965 (SP)
Recording data: 16, 20 & 29 October 1965, EMI Studios, London
Producer: George Martin
Engineer: Norman Smith

"The lyrics might have been personal. It is often a good way to work your own thoughts out. It saves you going to a psychiatrist, you allow yourself to say what you might not say in person." – **Paul McCartney**

"Day Tripper was based on an old folk song I wrote about a month previous. It was very hard going that, and it sounds it. It wasn't a serious message song. It was a drug song." – **John Lennon**

The first ever "double A-sided" single, recorded during the sessions for the *Rubber Soul* album, released on the same day.

It was also the first record supported by bespoke promotional videos (or 'filmed inserts', as they were then called). The band in fact recorded a total of five such films in one day in November at Twickenham Film Studios (the other three songs were 'Help!', 'Ticket To Ride' and 'I Feel Fine').

In these pre-MTV days, the idea was to simply avoid making personal appearances and still be seen worldwide with very little effort. It worked a treat, but then both of these songs were pretty awesome and would surely have been the big success they were with the littlest advertising campaign.

Even to this day, I can't decide which the better song is. The opening riff to 'Day Tripper' really mesmerised me at the time, and I of course had no idea that it was written on (and about) drugs. Nor did I understand what the line "she's a big teaser" inferred – indeed, not until I heard Jimi Hendrix's *BBC* session version many years later (where it is more explicitly sung, though not with Lennon as has been insinuated) did it hit me.

That both songs were hastily co-composed to meet a deadline is astonishing. While it's fair to say that Lennon came up with the idea for 'Day Tripper' and McCartney initiated 'We Can Work It Out', these are true collaborations that show the partnership nearing its creative peak. Not long after, most regular folk would be able to discern who had written what – "Oh, that's one of Paul's..." blah-blah – for the most part because they would sing the lead and their individual voices were now becoming more distinctive. That they both continue to make contributions to one another's songs is not in doubt. Nor that they would each try and outdo the other. But they were now both in (but not necessarily enjoying!) long-term relationships, with differing outside influences, getting more involved with drugs and no longer constantly huddled together in the back of the bus or sitting eye to eye cranking them out.

Of 'We Can Work It Out', Lennon said "Paul did the first half, I did the middle eight. But you've got Paul writing, 'We can work it out, we can work it out' - real optimistic, y'know, and me impatient: 'Life is very short and there's no time for fussing and fighting, my friend.'" So clearly their outlook was becoming slightly at odds too. Yes, the times they were a-changing, and from hereon in, McCartney would start to emerge as the band's musical leader.

Harrison was credited with helping on the arrangement for the song, but not sufficiently to allow for a co-credit. Lennon plays harmonium during the verses and they all clearly put a little more effort into this side of the single, which Epstein decreed the more commercial.

But better than 'Day Tripper'? Ask me again... in a few years, yeah?

RUBBER SOUL

UK Release: Parlophone PMC 1267 (mono) / PCS 3075 (stereo), 3 December 1965 (LP)
US Release: Capitol T-2442 (mono) / ST-2442 (stereo), 6 December 1965 (LP)
Recording data: 17 June & 12 October – 11 November 1965, EMI Studios, London
Producer: George Martin
Engineer: Norman Smith
Tracks: Drive My Car / Norwegian Wood (This Bird Has Flown) / You Won't See Me / Nowhere Man / Think For Yourself / The Word / Michelle / What Goes On / Girl / I'm Looking Through You / In My Life / Wait / If I Needed Someone / Run For Your Life

---

"Rubber Soul really was a matter of having all experienced the recording studio and having grown musically as well, but mainly having experienced the studio and knowing the possibilities." – **John Lennon**

Although this was their second album of all originals, it was the first one on which they truly asserted themselves, taking control of the studio, their instruments, the arrangements - even the front cover. As Lennon commented, "In the early days, we had to take what we were given, we didn't know how you can get more bass. We were learning the technique on *Rubber Soul*. We were more precise about making the album." The divide between Lennon and McCartney songs was becoming ever more evident here – with Lennon's first-person lyrics ('Norwegian Wood', 'In My Life') and McCartney's more light-hearted pop ('Drive My Car') and melodic balladeering '(Michelle').

But that's not to say that McCartney wasn't capable of writing from the heart: 'You Won't See Me' and 'I'm Looking Through You' touch on his then troubled relationship with actress Jane Asher. And Lennon in turn was far from averse to taking things too seriously: in response to false accusations of hidden lewdness in earlier recordings, he had McCartney and Harrison repeat the word "tit" in their backing vocals on 'Girl'.

The Beatles were now noticeably moving towards being a studio band, with the album utilising sitar (played by Harrison), fuzz bass (McCartney), harmonium (Lennon), a pack of matches (Starr – no, really!) and tape trickery (courtesy producer Martin) to create music that couldn't easily be replicated in a live environment.

Rubber Soul also saw a greater influence of contemporaries, like Bob Dylan and The Byrds, on the group's songwritng – indeed, Harrison's 'If I Needed Someone' is clearly a nod towards The Byrds' 'The Bells Of Rhymney'.

Paradoxically, a cover of 'If I Needed Someone' was issued as a single by 'Manchester Beatles' The Hollies on the same day as *Rubber Soul*, and failed to get into the top ten. This resulted in some disharmony between the *Parlophone* label-mates.

Earlier influences were naturally still in evidence. The album's closer clearly borrows from Elvis Presley's 1955 hit, 'Baby, Let's Play House', though Lennon was later to dismiss 'Run For Your Life' as a 'knock-off. But in 1965, he had no qualms about criticising McCartney for his original 'crap' lyrics to 'Drive My Car', and coercing his partner to do better.

On 'Norwegian Wood', the married Lennon was "trying to write about an affair without letting my wife know," (His six-year marriage to Cynthia Powell would be officially dissolved three years later.) Musically, it is famed for being the first example of a rock band using a sitar in one of their songs. Harrison bought the instrument after 'messing around' with one during a scene in *Help!*. He taught himself to how play it, and Lennon asked him to use it on this song. Lennon was seemingly less than enthused by Harrison's performance on acoustic guitar, though, and his demonstration of how he wanted it to sound ended up being used on the finished recording.

'Nowhere Man' was the Beatles' first non-love song, rather ironically written by Lennon while taking a break after getting nowhere trying to write a song. Yet another first was Starr's writing credit – together with Lennon and McCartney – on 'What Goes On'. He said no matter how hard he tried, he just couldn't write full songs then. So his contribution was no more than a few words. But it was clear evidence that, with Harrison also getting two of his own songs on an album again, the main songwriters were keen to ensure harmony in the ranks.

Arguably the strongest track on *Rubber Soul* is 'In My Life', which Lennon (with a little help from McCartney) composed after being urged to write about his childhood. Honing his writing skills, he whittled down a 'boring poem' to this two and a half minute slice of sweet melancholia that Lennon would drolly regard as one "of the ones that stand out a bit". This is helped no end by George Martin's Baroque-sounding piano solo.

American Beatles' releases were still out of sync with the UK, and *Rubber Soul* in the States was intentionally marketed as a more 'folk rock' album, with 'I've Just Seen A Face' and 'It's Only Love' from *Help!* replacing some of the more upbeat tracks. On both sides of the Atlantic, the double A-sided single 'We Can Work It Out'/'Day Tripper' was issued at the same time as the album, demonstrating what a spectacularly productive year 1965 had been for the group.

The album was released the same day the band commenced their last ever UK concert tour.

THE BEATLES' MILLION SELLERS

UK Release: Parlophone GEP 8946, 6 December 1965 (EP)
Recording data: 1963 & 1964, EMI Studios, London and Pathé Marconi Studios, Paris.
Producer: George Martin
Engineer: Norman Smith
Tracks: She Loves You / I Want To Hold Your Hand / Can't Buy Me Love / I Feel Fine

---

A mono-only collation of four singles that had each sold over one million copies. Why the heck would anyone want to buy them again? It topped the charts for four weeks in 1966, thus proving I know absolutely nowt. Or that the Beatles truly were a phenomenon. Take your pick.

BEATLES '65

US Release: Capitol ST-2228, 15 December 1965 (LP)
Recording data: June–October 1964, EMI Studios, London
Producer: George Martin
Engineer: Norman Smith
Tracks: No Reply / I'm A Loser / Baby's In Black / Rock And Roll Music / I'll Follow The Sun / Mr. Moonlight / Honey Don't / I'll Be Back / She's A Woman / I Feel Fine / Everybody's Trying To Be My Baby

---

Capitol misleadingly title yet another album, as all of the tracks here were recorded in 1964. But at just 26 minutes long, that should be the least of anyone's quibbles.

So you can clearly see what Harrison was talking about when he said they released more albums in the States. But that's not to say that the *Capitol* albums are in any way sonically or musically inferior. Just shorter, and not in line with the artist's original intent. And furthermore, there are thousands of North American fans who grew up listening to the band's recordings in this configuration and wouldn't want it any other way.

Vive la difference, I guess.

THE BEATLES' THIRD CHRISTMAS RECORD

UK Release: Lyntone LYN 948, 17 December 1965 (SP)
Recording data: 8 November 1965, Dick James Music, London
Producer: Tony Barrow

With 'Yesterday' being the first Beatles song to feature just one band member, the other boys get to right things here with short off-key a cappella renditions throughout this disc. As before, they thank the fans for the presents they've sent them throughout the year - like masticated chewing gum and knickers - and Lennon sings his ditty 'Happy Christmas To Ya List'nas'. They frequently lapse into heavy scouse accents and recite an original poem called Christmas Comes But Once a Year, as their humourous ad-libs shine through the holes in Barrow's skeleton of a script

US fan-club members did not receive this flexi-disc in '65 because the tape arrived too late; they had to make do with a black and white postcard instead. They was robbed. Again.

YESTERDAY

UK Release: Parlophone GEP 8948, 4 March 1966 (EP)
Recording data: 1965, EMI Studios, London.
Producer: George Martin
Engineer: Norman Smith
Tracks: Yesterday / Act Naturally / You Like Me Too Much / It's Only Love

---

Notable mainly for the fact that each of the tracks featured have the lads taking a turn at singing the lead vocals. That is all.

PAPERBACK WRITER / RAIN

UK Release: Parlophone R 5452, 30 May 1966 (SP)
US Release: Capitol 5651, 30 May 1966 (SP)
Recording data: 13 & 14 April 1966, EMI Studios, London
Producer: George Martin
Engineer: Geoff Emerick

"Paperback Writer is son of Day Tripper, but it is Paul's song. Son of Day Tripper meaning a rock 'n' roll song with a guitar lick on a fuzzy, loud guitar." – **John Lennon**

This was the single that made people realise that McCartney was more than just a pretty face – largely due to his first use of a *Rickenbacker* guitar, how it was recorded and the way in which the record was mastered. As engineer Emerick commented, it "was the first time the bass sound had been heard in all its excitement".

The band again made promotional films for both sides of the single. These were directed by Michael Lindsay-Hogg, who would continue to work with the band thereafter, including his helming of their final feature length film, *Let It Be*. He would also be regularly employed by the Rolling Stones post this, and would go on to work with McCartney throughout the 70s.

In the films, the result of a moped accident McCartney suffered on Boxing Day 1965 is clearly visible: a chipped front tooth and scarred upper lip (the small bump of which can still be seen to this day). McCartney had hired a couple of mopeds to visit relatives in the Wirral with his friend, Tara Browne – a heir to the Guinness fortune. Almost a year later, Browne was involved in another accident, this time when his sports car crashed into the side of a parked lorry at high speed in South Kensington. Unfortunately, the crash proved fatal, and Lennon would be inspired to pen a verse about this in 'A Day In The Life'. (Yes, sadly Browne didn't notice that the lights had changed.)

Possibly because the lyrics to 'Paperback Writer' actually refers to the newspaper, many years from then McCartney would claim that the idea for this song came to him after reading an article about "people writing paperbacks" in the sodding *Daily Mail*.

Actually, it should be noted that the newspaper was still a broadsheet then and, in those pre-Leveson days, its editor issued instructions to his journalists stipulating that "no member of the *Daily Mail* staff intrudes or is called upon to intrude into private lives where no public interest is involved." And, further, that "no ordinary member of the public is lured, coerced or in any way pressed by a *Daily Mail* representative into giving an interview or picture which he is clearly unwilling to give."

Those days are sadly long gone, and today the rag has to be one of the worst tabloids we have.

But could McCartney possibly have misremembered the song's origin? According to music journalist Steve Turner (in his fab book, *A Hard Day's Write*, documenting "the stories behind every Beatles song"), that notorious arbiter of good taste and upholder of all that is decent, the late Sir James Wilson Vincent Savile OBE KCSG told him that he was backstage with the band when the idea for the single was first conceived. Posthumously disgraced DJ Savile claimed that one of McCartney's aunties had asked him to write a song that wasn't about love for a change. Starr happened to be reading a paperback, and McCartney "announced that he would write a song about a book."

How's about that then, guys and gals? As the lyrics reference "the dirty story of a dirty man", it would perhaps be more appropriate if Savile's version of events were true.

It takes the form of a letter to a potential publisher, and was a further attempt to write a one-note song (like 'Long Tall Sally' and 'The Word'). They embellished it in the studio with some typically great four-part harmony vocals, and Lennon and Harrison sang the French nursery rhyme Frère Jacques in the background.

If anyone ever slags off Starr's abilities as a drummer, they've clearly never listened to 'Rain'. And when they have, you must point out to 'em that Starr actually played it faster than you hear, as they slowed the rhythm track recording down after.

A song in praise of precipitation following the torrential rain the band encountered when they landed in Melbourne, Australia. The song is also thought to be influenced by trip-trip-tripping on LSD, but how would I know? Musically and technically it's of far greater significance, however - principally because the lyrics of the final verse are played backwards.

Said Lennon, "After we'd done the session, I went home with a tape to see what else you could do with it. And I was sort of very tired, you know, not knowing what I was doing, and I just happened to put it on my own tape recorder and it came out backwards. And I liked it better."

Lennon had wanted to have the song entirely this way, but that was a little too radical. At least, for now. But it did lead to further experiments with backward tapes on the next album.

YESTERDAY... AND TODAY

US Release: Capitol ST-2553, 20 June 1966 (LP)
Recording data: 1965–1966, EMI Studios, London
Producer: George Martin
Engineer: Norman Smith
Tracks: Drive My Car / I'm Only Sleeping / Nowhere Man / Doctor Robert / Yesterday / Act Naturally / And Your Bird Can Sing / If I Needed Someone / We Can Work It Out / What Goes On / Day Tripper

---

The final album compiled by *Capitol* for the North American market, and one that again pipped us British by including three songs from the band's next proper album (*Revolver*).

As noted in my introduction, the band were increasingly pissed off by *Capitol's* meddling, and after this and their butchering of *Revolver*, they put their foot down with a firm hand.

The big story here is the original cover shot by photographer Robert Whitaker, who had befriended the band – and in particular, Lennon – while they toured Australia. Epstein invited Whitaker to become staff photographer at NEMS, and he would gain unlimited access to the boys for a couple of years, including snapping them during their second US tour. (He also accompanied The Beatles on their 1966 tour of Japan and took the colour photo of the group inspecting antiques used on the back cover of the *A Collection of Beatles Oldies* album.)

Fed up with having to do another photo session for their upcoming single, the band agreed to try something a little different at Whitaker's Chelsea studio. "Bob was into Dali and making surreal pictures," said Lennon.

In 1991, Whitaker told *Goldmine* magazine, "I wanted to do a real experiment – people will jump to wrong conclusions about it being sick, but the whole thing is based on simplicity – linking four very real people with something real. I got George to knock some nails into John's head, and took some sausages along to get some other pictures, dressed them up in white smocks as butchers, and this is the result - the use of the camera as a means of creating situations."

In the shot are dismembered doll parts, false teeth and lumps of meat, with the lads all grinning away (it would be a few years before Harrison and McCartney would become vegetarians). The photo appeared first in the UK – essentially to promote the 'Paperback Writer' single - with little or no reaction. Apparently McCartney then pushed for it to be used as an album cover in the US – describing it as "our comment on the war" in Vietnam. *Capitol* duly pressed several hundred thousand copies of the album in the 'butcher' sleeve, and off they went. The outcry was instantaneous, and *EMI* chairman Sir Joseph Lockwood ordered all copies to be shipped back to *Capitol*, making it highly collectable.

An uncontentious alternate shot by Whitaker, showing the lads around an open travelling chest, was pasted over many of the returned records. And this – the 'trunk' cover – would become the official sleeve for all subsequent reissues.

NOWHERE MAN

UK Release: Parlophone GEP 8952, 8 July 1966 (EP)
Recording data: 1965, EMI Studios, London.
Producer: George Martin
Engineer: Norman Smith
Tracks: Nowhere Man / Drive My Car / Michelle / You Won't See Me

---

Notable for being the last collection of cuts culled from an album and dumped on an extended player to fleece the kids, man. At least in the UK, and while the band was still active.

And this wasn't the only way record companies tried to capitalise on the band's phenomenal success; other bands were encouraged to quickly produce cover versions of new Beatles' songs to achieve instant success. One such band was the Overlanders, who recorded 'Michelle' and got it to number one in the UK singles chart one month after *Rubber Soul* had been released - just pipping a rival cover by David and Jonathan.

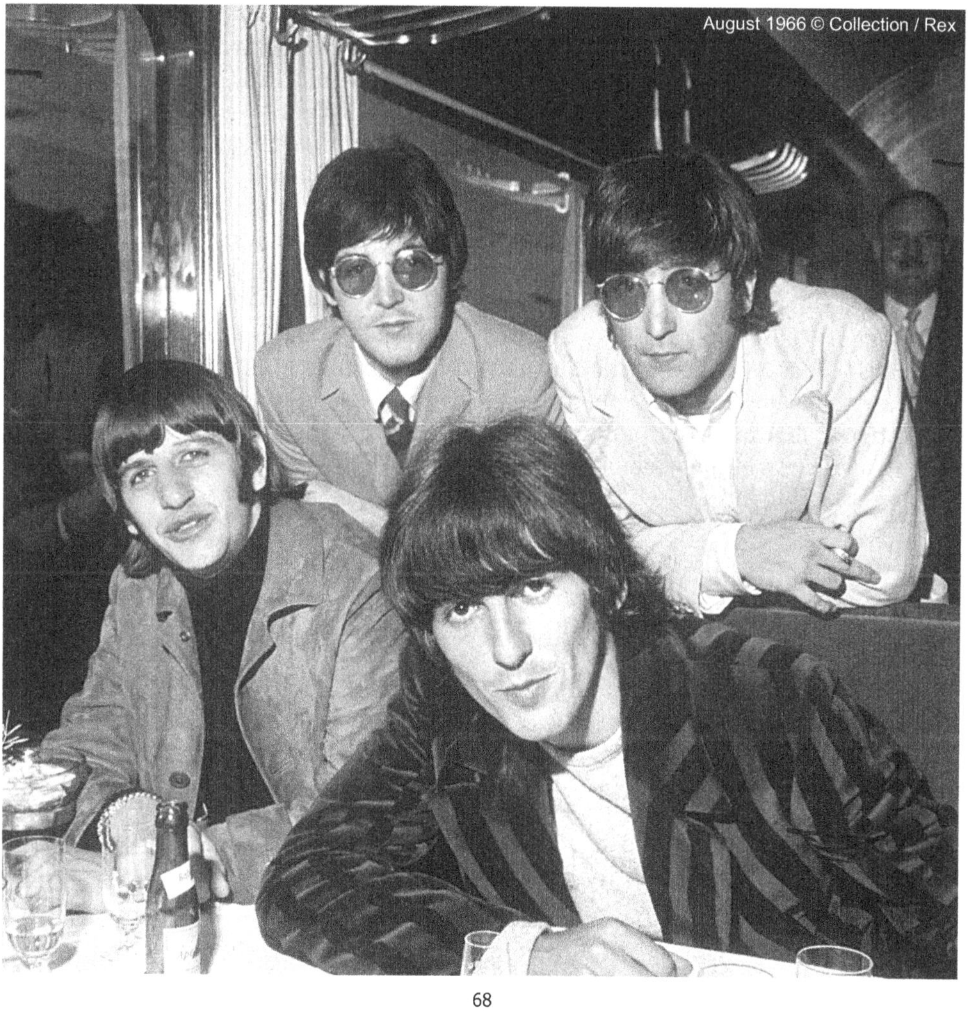
August 1966 © Collection / Rex

YELLOW SUBMARINE / ELEANOR RIGBY

UK Release: Parlophone R 5493, 5 August 1966 (SP)
US Release: Capitol 5715, 8 August 1966 (SP)
Recording data: 28–29 April, 26 May, 1 and 6 June 1966, EMI Studios, London
Producer: George Martin
Engineer: Geoff Emerick

"With 'Yellow Submarine', the whole idea was, 'if someday I came across some kids singing it, that will be it,' so it's got to be very easy. There isn't a single big word. Kids will understand it easier than adults" – **Paul McCartney**

Released on the same day as the album *Revolver*, from which both songs are taken.

Many people diss McCartney for songs like 'Yellow Submarine', but he openly admitted he was trying to write a children's song. Same with 'We All Stand Together' (aka The Frog Song) many years later. And children do love 'em. Mission accomplished. Go fuck yourselves if you can't take a joke.

Starr (who sang the song) confirmed there were "no hidden meanings. Many people have interpreted it to be a war song, that eventually all the world would be living in yellow submarines. That's not the case."

A simple story that kids can relate to. When I was at school, because there were so few instruments to play and we were all pretty inept musically, our music lessons consisted of our teacher, Mrs Snelson, playing the likes of 'I'm Henery The Eighth', I Am', 'Football Crazy' and 'Yellow Submarine' on the piano, while we all sang along. For the bit where the brass band began to play during 'Yellow Submarine', Mrs Snelson would whistle while we tried to stifle our guffaws. Aah, jumpers for goalposts. And C minus marks all round from Mrs S on our end of year reports. Happy days.

Of course, many years later, 'I'm Henery The Eighth, I Am' would have a son he named Will.

'Eleanor Rigby' was the first Beatles record not to feature any of the band as musicians – just a double string quartet played Martin's masterly arrangement of McCartney's music. Add lyrics about the elderly and loneliness, and you see why the Beatles truly shattered the pop-group mould they'd helped create. McCartney was inspired to use a string quartet following his introduction to the music of Italian Baroque composer, Antonio Vivaldi (who famously wrote *The Four Seasons*.

REVOLVER

UK Release: Parlophone PMC 7009 (mono) / PCS 7009 (stereo), 5 August 1966 (LP)
US Release: Capitol T-2576 (mono) / ST-2576 (stereo), 8 August 1966 (LP)
Recording data: 6 April – 22 June 1966, EMI Studios, London
Producer: George Martin
Engineer: Geoff Emerick, Peter Vince
Tracks: Taxman / Eleanor Rigby / I'm Only Sleeping / Love You To / Here, There And Everywhere / Yellow Submarine / She Said She Said / Good Day Sunshine / And Your Bird Can Sing / For No One / Doctor Robert / I Want To Tell You / Got To Get You Into My Life / Tomorrow Never Knows

---

"We were going to record Revolver in America, but they wanted a fantastic amount of money to use the facilities there. We thought we'd forget it because they were obviously trying to take us for a ride because we were The Beatles. We'd been thinking about going to record there for some time. When we finished Revolver, we realised that we had found a new British sound almost by accident. I think there were only two tracks on the LP that would have sounded better if we'd cut them in America. 'Taxman' and 'Got To Get You Into My Life' because they need that raw quality that you just can't get in this country for some reason. But 'Eleanor Rigby' would have been worse, because the string players in America aren't so good. We may still record in America. What we might do though is write some numbers especially, take them over, do them and see how it works." – **Paul McCartney**

A game-changer in many ways, not least because it marked the very last time the US would fanny around with a Beatles album (though they did later transform an EP into a long player) and start issuing them as was, as is, and as shall forever after be, as nature intended. Sadly, though, instead of adding tracks to its version of *Revolver, Capitol* simply removed the three songs they had already plundered for *Yesterday... And Today* - 'I'm Only Sleeping', 'And Your Bird Can Sing' and 'Doctor Robert' – making it a 28 minute, eleven track album, and one with Harrison being the principal writer of one more song than Lennon.

Following the appearance of a string quartet on 'Yesterday' and a flautist on 'You've Got To Hide Your Love Away', this album saw even greater use of outsiders with more strings and aerophones as well as tape manipulation and the band themselves experimenting on a wider range of instruments.

Although at the time of its release, the band was still touring and playing the old hits on auto-pilot, their restlessness manifested itself here on this studio album where, for the first time, none of the songs would be performed live. Their whole outlook was changing, as exemplified by the opening track from Harrison, 'Taxman'.

"I had discovered I was paying a huge amount of money to the taxman. You are so happy that you've finally started earning money - and then you find out about tax. In those days we paid 19 shillings and sixpence out of every pound, and with supertax and surtax and tax-tax it was ridiculous - a heavy penalty to pay for making money." And so Harrison penned his attack on the Treasury, which heralded another first for the band by explicitly naming two living individuals: Harold Wilson (who was Prime Minister of the UK at the time) and Ted Heath (who would succeed Wilson four years later). It was the first time the band had really commented on current affairs too, albeit without offering a solution and blithely pointing the finger at both the current Government and Her Majesty's Most Loyal Opposition. Bloody liberals.

The song is counted in by Lennon (according to Harrison, in the letters page of issue 41 of The Beatles Monthly Book), who also plays the very fine lead guitar solo, about which Harrison said, "I was pleased to have Paul play that bit... if you notice, he did like a little Indian bit on it for me." With Harrison playing the distorted rhythm guitar throughout, Lennon was relegated to backing vocalist, though he did grudgingly assist Harrison with a few uncredited one-liners.

Lennon's 'I'm Only Sleeping' came about as a result of his habitual marathon kips, out of which he needed to be awoken by McCartney so they could write together. The song features a reversed guitar duet by Harrison, who wrote out his planned solo, then reversed this notation and performed and recorded it twice. The tapes were then reversed to create the desired effect.

After adding some sitar to 'Norwegian Wood', Harrison wanted to write a tune that was specifically for the sitar. The words to 'Love You To' speak about his recently wed wife, Pattie. The track featured just two Fabs: its author on multi-tracked lead vocals, acoustic guitar, fuzz electric guitar, bass and sitar, and Mr Starr on tambourine. They were supported by Indian session musicians on tabla, tambura and sitar. McCartney contributed falsetto harmonies, but these had been dumped by the time of the final mix.

Next comes the first of two absolute belters from McCartney. Written besides Lennon's swimming pool at his house in Weybridge, 'Here, There and Everywhere' was practically finished by the time the homeowner woke up. It's hard to believe that a 23 year old could come up with such a mature love song, but then Jane Asher was a right bird - though I'm pretty sure she never worked at the pickle factory with our Reg, or had a mate whose stockings fell down when she sang 'Anyone Who Had A Heart'. Whatever, Lennon and McCartney seem to agree that this was the best song on the album. Me, I'm not so sure, but it's very close and shows that McCartney was upping his game after Lennon's forays away from teeny-pleasing, with songs like 'In My Life'.

'She Said, She Said' came about because of something a stoned pre-Easy Rider Peter Fonda said. The band were on a break from their summer 1965 tour of the US at a rented house in Beverly Hills, taking LSD – except McCartney. Fonda, the son of Henry/younger brother of Jane, was invited to join the band, along with Roger McGuinn and David Crosby of The Byrds.

On his eleventh birthday, Fonda had accidentally shot himself in the stomach with a (cough) revolver, and nearly died. In his wasted state, and in a bid to calm a freaked out Harrison (who was probably worried about having nicked McGuinn's riff from 'The Bells Of Rhymney'), Fonda kept repeating that he knew what it was like to be dead. Lennon asked him to shut up, later saying, "We didn't want to hear about that! We were on an acid trip and the sun was shining and the girls were dancing and the whole thing was really beautiful and Sixties. And this guy - who I really didn't know - kept coming over, and we kept leaving him because he was so boring. It was scary, when you're flying high: 'Don't tell me about it. I don't want to know what it's like to be dead!'" Harrison would say that Fonda was "very uncool", insisting upon showing them his bullet wound. But, nevertheless, a song was born.

And it was to be the final song recorded for *Revolver*, only added when they realised they were running short. I wonder, would *Capitol* have gotten away with an even shorter album had they not added this at the eleventh hour?

Harrison claims he helped Lennon stitch the piece together, and it was rehearsed and recorded in one marathon nine-hour session by the band – except McCartney. After it was done, Martin apparently had to go and have a lie down, as he'd also been working on the album's final mono and stereo mixes.

'She Said, She Said' was followed by a song inspired by The Lovin' Spoonful's 'Daydream', which was on the charts at the time the *Revolver* album was being recorded.

John Sebastian, who wrote that song, later commented, "One of the wonderful things The Beatles had going for them is that they were so original that when they did cop an idea from somebody else it never occurred to you. I thought there were one or two of their songs which were Spoonful-oid but it wasn't until Paul mentioned it in a *Playboy* interview that I specifically realised we'd inspired 'Good Day Sunshine'."

Incidentally, The Lovin' Spoonful got their name from Mississippi John Hurt's 'Coffee Blues', a song of praise for a nice cup of *Maxwell House*. It has nothing to do with the amount of semen in an average male ejaculation. Ditto the name 10CC, which came to Jonathan King in a dream. If anyone tells you different, they're tossers.

Right, back to 'Good Day Sunshine', which was mainly penned by McCartney and is one of the more cheerful songs on the album (there was a marked change in the happy/sad ratio of the songs here). Lyrically 'Good Day Sunshine' had nowt to do with greed or death, but rather a walk in the park with Jane Asher. Ahh, how sweet!

And 'Your Bird Can Sing' was chiefly composed by Lennon and features a driving dual-guitar melody performed live (with no overdubs) by Harrison and McCartney. Originally titled 'You Don't Get Me', it is believed that the lyrics refer to Mick Jagger and his then girlfriend, Marianne Faithfull. The English singer, songwriter and actress had had a minor hit in 1965 with the song 'This Little Bird', so who knows? LSD may also have had a hand in its creation, though.

And so to the second McCartney belter: 'For No One', which Lennon readily admitted was one of his favourites by his songwriting partner, and for me is the best song on *Revolver*. Initially named 'Why Did It Die?', it tells of the end of a relationship in which the female protagonist no longer needs the male, yet still she cries: for no one. McCartney believes he wrote it following an argument with Asher while on a skiing holiday in the Swiss Alps, so again it's very far from being an upbeat piece. But great music does not have to be cheerful to be uplifting.

McCartney had the idea of having a French Horn play the song's solo, which he sang for Martin to transcribe for 'the best horn player in London', one Alan Civil. The brass player's contribution adds to the overall tone of the piece, though Civil downplayed the significance of his contribution by saying it was "just another day's work, the third session that day in fact." That he'd been coerced into playing a note beyond the usual range of the instrument was clearly of no never mind. That he'd played on, and helped enhance, one of the Fabs' more magnificent songs was astonishing.

The song's composer added a distinctive clavichord to his and Starr's rhythm track and, as was now fast becoming accepted practice, no other Beatles' were judged necessary to complete the tune.

Although Lennon would claim that 'Doctor Robert' was about himself - "I was the one that carried all the pills on tour and always have done," - the titular physician was undoubtedly Dr Robert Freymann, also known as the Great White Father. Dr Robert ran a discreet clinic in New York, which had a reputation for giving monied Manhattanites vitamin B-12 injections containing large doses of amphetamines. McCartney backed this up when he said, "We'd hear people say, 'You can get anything off him, any pills you want.' The song was a joke about this fellow who cured everyone of everything with all these pills and tranquilizers. He kept New York high." The song itself was one of the lesser tracks here, but is noteworthy for the band's most explicit mention of drug use to date as well as Harrison's sublime performance on maracas.

It seems Harrison came up with his song titles very late in the day around this period: 'Love You To' had the working title Granny Smith, so engineer Emerick jokingly named 'I Want To Tell You' after a classic old Victorian British apple: a Laxton's Superb.

A Granny Smith would later become the logo for the band's *Apple Records*, which was eventually appropriated by *Apple Inc.* - over Neil Aspinall's dead body. But what's that got to do with 'I Want To Tell You'? Well, as Harrison said, the song is "about the avalanche of thoughts that are so hard to write down or say or transmit." And that's what I'm having, alright? 'I Want To Tell You' was another reason why the subsequent studio album would top *Revolver*: yes, it's a decent enough tune but had they released this with 'Dr Robert' instead of the 'Paperback Writer' single – well, this was clearly considered not good enough to be a 45. And it doesn't come close to Harrison's 'Taxman'. McCartney played the distinctive piano pattern throughout on the initial backing tracks and later overdubbed his bass track. Meanwhile, Lennon snatched the maracas away from the song's composer in a fit of pique. Possibly.

Surprisingly, the final two tracks on *Revolver* were the first two recorded. And they are two of the better songs, with one each by Lennon and McCartney. 'Got to Get You Into My Life' is a song "that's directly about pot", McCartney admitted, and claimed that the song might have sounded better if recorded in the US because it needed "that raw quality that you just can't get in this country for some reason." The British brass section used, featuring two members of Georgie Fame's shortly to be disbanded Blue Flames, certainly did a fine job in capturing a Stax-like sound. And, as McCartney acknowledged, recording tracks like 'Eleanor Rigby' in America might not have worked out quite so well.

The band's original contract with *EMI* expired in June 1966 while they were recording *Revolver*, and they didn't renew it again until January 1967. So while they did apparently briefly ponder recording in the States, we can now only speculate on whether things would have sounded any different: the vast bulk of the band's core catalogue ended up being recorded in foggy London town.

To think that just four years previous, the Beatles were knocking out simple ditties like 'Love Me Do' beggars belief when you hear the last track here. They certainly didn't rest on their laurels, no siree. 'Tomorrow Never Knows' is easily the least conventional and most pioneering song on *Revolver*, so it is perhaps surprising that, as the first song recorded, the band didn't let their freak flag fly a little higher.

It was their first song to feature flanging, a sweeping artificial double-tracked effect created by engineer Ken Townsend, named by Lennon, and still very much in use today. There are also a number of tape loops used throughout the song: a distorted recording of McCartney laughing (the seagull sound); an orchestra playing a B flat chord; notes played on a Mellotron's flute and violin settings; a 'singing' wine glass; and a distorted sitar. But perhaps the most startling thing is the overall musical structure of the piece, which barely deviates from the chord of C, and Starr's repetitive non-standard drum pattern.

With the Beatles having already broken away from the traditional three-chord sequence exemplified in most blues and rock and roll songs - even soppy old 'She Loves You' featured a more complex chord progression - they were now showing how to make just one chord sound interesting.

The title of the song - like 'A Hard Day's Night' - was taken from one of Starr's malapropisms, uttered during an interview on *BBC* TV just after the band had returned from the US in 1964. The lyrics were inspired by LSD and Timothy Leary's book, *The Psychedelic Experience: A Manual Based On The Tibetan Book Of The Dead*. Lennon acquired a copy at London's Indica Bookshop, which was co-owned by John Dunbar, the soon to be estranged husband of Marianne Faithfull. Faithfull had made the decision to "get a Rolling Stone as a boyfriend. I slept with three and decided the lead singer was the best bet." She subsequently sang background vocals on 'Yellow Submarine' together with one of the three lucky Stones, Mr Brian Jones.

Earlier, I belittled the album's cover for being in black and white. That was just to make a point, alright? The iconic front cover collage (for that's what it is) was created by the Beatles' old friend from Hamburg days, Klaus Voormann. He had moved to London and recently married *Coronation Street* actress, Christine Hargreaves. (A short time later, he would become Manfred Mann's bass player.)

Before making his first sketch, the band played Voormann 'Tomorrow Never Knows'. He would later comment that "They were being so avant-garde, I thought the cover has to do the same thing. How far can I go? How surreal and strange can it be?" In among the many images of the four Beatles, Voormann managed to weave in, in Harrison's hair, a photo of himself. The man who was to become Led Zeppelin's tour manager, Richard Cole, claims Lennon and Starr can be seen wearing shirts that he designed. Unfortunately, the drawings in the centre make the band look a little like The Rolling Stones. But overall, Voormann created something pretty special for a very special album. And won the Grammy Award for 'Best Album Cover, Graphic Arts' for his trouble. It is said that his old muckers paid him just £40 for his work, but the resultant interest and kudos from his association with the album and the band far outweigh any monetary considerations, surely?

So, a truly groundbreaking album, most certainly (as Sir Alf Ramsey was wont to say), but even better was to come... no, don't speak!

The album was released a week after England won the FIFA World Cup (for the first and only time), two days after the death of American satirist Lenny Bruce (who at the time was fighting a conviction for obscenity; he would receive a posthumous pardon in 2003), and on the very day that US teen mag DATEbook reprinted a quote from Lennon that the Beatles were now "more popular than Jesus" (a comment that caused no public reaction in good old Blighty when it first appeared in the London *Evening Standard* five months previously).

Conceptual artist Yoko Ono, who visited London the following month, says "World War II was still fresh in English minds," so the fact that England beat Germany in the final possibly heightened the feeling of elation in the Beatles' home country, where the album stayed at the top of the charts for seven weeks.

A COLLECTION OF BEATLES OLDIES

UK Release: Parlophone PMC 7016 (mono) / PCS 7016 (stereo), 10 December 1966 (LP)
Recording data: 1963–1966, EMI Studios, London and Pathé Marconi Studio, Paris
Producer: George Martin
Engineer: Norman Smith, Geoff Emerick
Tracks: She Loves You / From Me to You / We Can Work It Out / Help! / Michelle / Yesterday / I Feel Fine / Yellow Submarine / Can't Buy Me Love / Bad Boy / Day Tripper / A Hard Day's Night / Ticket to Ride / Paperback Writer / Eleanor Rigby / I Want to Hold Your Hand

---

All *EMI* wanted for Christmas was a new Beatles album - in its absence, they released this set of tracks recorded by the band during the last four years. The sole 'new' track was a cover of Larry Williams' 'Bad Boy', which had been recorded for the American market and had only previously appeared on *Capitol's Beatles VI.*

A Collection Of Beatles Oldies contained eight singles that were issued on LP for the first time in the UK - some in stereo mixes prepared especially for this compilation.

In spite of all this thrilling wonderment, it was the first Beatles album that failed to make it to number one. Nothing could knock the soundtrack to *The Sound Of Music* off the top slot that Christmas. Even men in the midst of a table d'hote heard that.

The album was issued six days before the UK release of the Jimi Hendrix Experience's first single, 'Hey Joe'.

THE BEATLES' FOURTH CHRISTMAS RECORD – PANTOMIME: EVERYWHERE IT'S CHRISTMAS

UK Release: Lyntone LYN 1145, 16 December 1966 (SP)
Recording data: 25 November 1966, Dick James Music Office, London
Producer: George Martin

Recorded between sessions for the group's next single, having Martin in the chair served to make this offering far less amateurish than hitherto.

With cover artwork by McCartney, the whole package clearly reflected the band's increasing sophistication (in the studio and elsewhere) and eschewed the traditional Barrow-encouraged seasonal greetings in favour of a collection of comic skits (like Felpin Mansions and the ever so slightly creepy Podgy The Bear And Jasper). Mixing in original songs (including 'Everywhere It's Christmas', 'Orowainya' and 'Please Don't Bring Your Banjo Back') helped make this a must-have stocking filler.

Sadly, US fan-club members missed out again, getting a postcard instead.

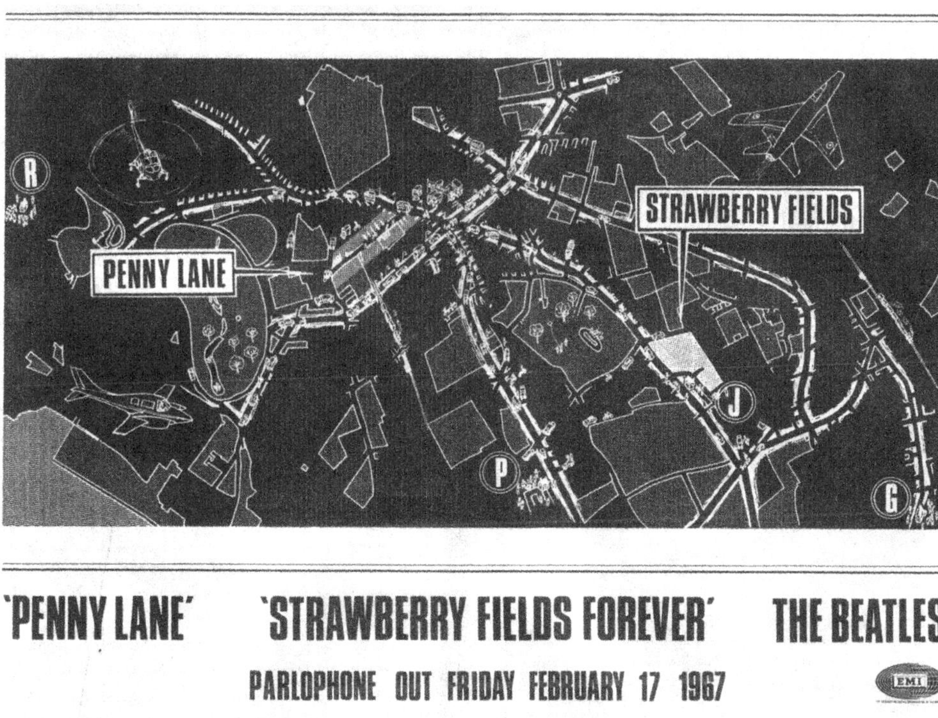

CARNIVAL OF LIGHT

UK Release: premiered at London's Roundhouse on 28 January 1967, otherwise unreleased (CP)
Recording data: 5 January 1967, EMI Studios, London
Producer: George Martin
Engineer: Geoff Emerick

After the posthumous *Anthology* and live at the Beeb releases, there remains one recording by the Beatles that fans would dearly love to see officially released – the near 15 minute experimental piece, 'Carnival Of Light'.

In December 1966, McCartney was asked – possibly by underground writer Barry Miles – to contribute a free-form recording for a festival promoting electronic music at London's Roundhouse, organised by the designers Binder, Edwards & Vaughan.

During the vocal sessions for 'Penny Lane', McCartney spake unto the others, saying "'Look we've got half an hour before the session officially starts, would you mind terribly if I did this thing?' And they all just fell in with the spirit of it and I just said, 'Would you go on that and would you stay on that and would you be on that and we'll just take twenty minutes to do it in real time?' And they all just got into it."

The tape was then handed over to Binder, Edwards & Vaughan to be played at The Million Volt Light And Sound Rave (sometimes referred to as The Carnival Of Light Rave) on 28 January and 4 February 1967.

Vaughan thought McCartney "would make more of it than he did", and engineer Emerick commented that, after the session, Martin said to him, "This is ridiculous, we've got to get our teeth into something more constructive."

In his book *The Complete Beatles Recording Sessions*, Lewisohn writes that the song includes "distorted, hypnotic drum and organ sounds, various effects and Lennon and McCartney screaming dementedly and bawling aloud random phrases like 'Are you alright?' and 'Barcelona!'"

McCartney now claims it's "the coolest piece of music since sliced bread!" and harbours hopes of fully unveiling it to the public at large at some point in the future.

BEATLES PLAN TV SPEC FOR LP; NEXT SINGLE LONGEST-EVER ?

THE Beatles are likely to film their own TV spectacular soon, featuring the tracks from their next LP which is nearing completion. One track lasting more than four minutes is being considered for their next single. The Beatles' film plans are now taking shape.

The Beatles have resumed marathon recording sessions following the Christmas holidays. They are completing sufficient tracks for the single and the next album.

The LP will probably not be issued until March, but Brian Epstein revealed this week that the Beatles are already considering a plan to make a TV show built round the new songs — for network screening soon after release.

Epstein also disclosed that two already-recorded songs are strongly favoured for the next single to be issued at the end of January. The four-minute track is the longest-ever waxed by the Beatles.

"But they won't take a decision until they have recorded everything they have to do. We should know by next week," Epstein added.

Although the first draft of the script for the Beatles' next film has not met with their immediate approval, they are going ahead with writer Owen Holder and producer Walter Shenson on improvements, and Epstein said that production would begin "in the first half of 1967."

Meanwhile, negotiations for a film part for Ringo—first revealed in the NME on November 26—are definitely in progress.

PENNY LANE / STRAWBERRY FIELDS FOREVER

UK Release: Parlophone R 5570, 17 February 1967 (SP)
US Release: Capitol 5810, 13 February 1967 (SP)
Recording data: November 1966 – January 1967, EMI Studios, London
Producer: George Martin
Engineer: Geoff Emerick

"Most people wouldn't hear it, but 'finger pie' is just a nice little joke for the Liverpool lads who like a bit of smut." – **Paul McCartney**

"Strawberry Fields was psychoanalysis set to music. Dick Lester offered me the part in this movie, which gave me time to think without going home. We were in Almería, and it took me six weeks to write the song. As anybody knows about film work, there's a lot of hanging around." – **John Lennon**

Eight 'Grammies' for Beatles; Vaud award?

THE Beatles have been nominated in eight sections of America's Grammy Awards—the pop world's equivalent of Hollywood's Oscars. The awards are made annually by the National Academy of Recording Arts and Sciences, and the winners will be announced this year on March 2.

The New Vaudeville Band also figures in the nominations with its "Winchester Cathedral" listed in the Record of the Year section.

Most successful of the Beatles' songs is "Eleanor Rigby," which is nominated in four separate sections—Best Vocal Performance, Best Contemporary Record and Best Arrangement Accompanying a Vocal, also Record of the Year.

"Michelle" is nominated as Best Song of the Year and Best Instrumental Arrangement. The group's "Revolver" LP receives nominations as Best Album of the Year and Best Album Cover—the sleeve was designed by Klaus Voorman of the Manfred Mann group.

The Beatles won another Gold Disc this week, for "Penny Lane"/"Strawberry Fields Forever," before the record was actually on sale in the States. President of Capitol Records Alan Livingstone reported one million U.S. advance orders.

When my brother and I used to listen to this single – or any other record, for that matter – on our cheap little Dansette-copy portable record player, we used to lift the stylus off after the fade out. It wasn't until quite a few weeks after getting 'Strawberry Fields' – when my brother was out, and I was too busy to attend immediately to this menial task – that I heard the weird ending. It scared the shit out of me.

Amazingly, for what is arguably one of the finest couplings in the history of 45-rpm gramophone recordings, this was the Beatles' first single not to reach number one in the UK charts since their debut release ('Love Me Do' that is, not that one where they backed Tony Sheridan). These two fine pieces of music were kept off the top by the 2012 Eurovision song contest loser, Engelbert Humperdinck. But – and I cannot lie, this is a big but – only because, being a double A-side, sales were halved. Yes, split 50/50 between the pair. As was the way in those days. Outrageous.

SGT. PEPPER'S LONELY HEARTS CLUB BAND

UK Release: Parlophone PMC 7027 (mono) / PCS 7027 (stereo), 1 June 1967 (LP)
US Release: Capitol MAS-2653 (mono) / SMAS-2653 (stereo), 2 June 1967 (LP)
Recording data: 6 December 1966 – 21 April 1967, EMI and Regent Sound Studios, London
Producer: George Martin
Engineer: Geoff Emerick
Tracks: Sgt. Pepper's Lonely Hearts Club Band / With A Little Help From My Friends / Lucy In The Sky With Diamonds / Getting Better / Fixing A Hole / She's Leaving Home / Being For The Benefit Of Mr. Kite! / Within You Without You / When I'm Sixty-Four / Lovely Rita / Good Morning Good Morning / Sgt. Pepper's Lonely Hearts Club Band (Reprise) / A Day In The Life

---

"I made a suggestion. I said, we need to get away from ourselves. How about if we just become some sort of an alter-ego band?" – **Paul McCartney**

There are folk who claim that wherever you went in the long hot summer of 1967, you could hear this album playing. Certainly I saw the inside of the album sleeve in the window of the Kentish Times' office in Orpington High Street on its release, and wondered what had become of my beloved mop-tops. And I was far from being alone in becoming disillusioned with the boys. And so I didn't actually hear the whole thing until I was a teenager a few years later. Yes, it was only when I started listening to the likes of Deep Purple, Black Sabbath and Yes that I realised the full impact the band had had on my new heroes, and went back and discovered the band's most creative period.

But as it was, in 1967 this nine-year-old Greenaway was more interested in 45s and defacing his Beatles' Selcol New Sound toy guitar. Yeah, I scratched their faces from it. Not sure what became of it, but copies in good condition these days fetch a fair few bob on eBay. What a little tit.

Anyway, "Sgt. Pepper" is a pivotal album - not just for the Beatles, but for popular music in general. There are some – usually looking at things from the perspective of hindsight (hey, I quickly realised the error of my ways, okay?) – who argue till they're blue in the tits that *Revolver* is a superior album. But they're just being obtuse. Just look at the covers: monochrome versus multi-coloured. It's like saying *The Unforgettable Fire* is better than *The Joshua Tree*, that *Wish You Were Here* outshines *The Dark Side Of The Moon*, and *(What's the Story) Morning Glory?* is better than *Definitely Maybe*. Or even that *Desire* is superior to Blood On The Tracks... oh, hold on: I'm getting confused now. They're all great albums, aren't they? But get real and accept the blindingly obvious. Go on, do it. "Sgt. Pepper" is the Beatles' biggest selling album. It simply cannot be overrated. Even McCartney would claim it to be the band's *Freak Out!*, in deference to Frank Zappa's first magnum opus (yeah, he wrote a few!).

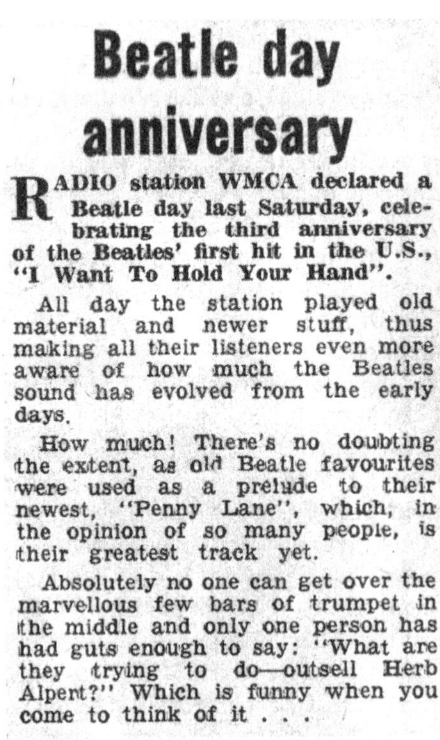

Beatle day anniversary

RADIO station WMCA declared a Beatle day last Saturday, celebrating the third anniversary of the Beatles' first hit in the U.S., "I Want To Hold Your Hand".

All day the station played old material and newer stuff, thus making all their listeners even more aware of how much the Beatles sound has evolved from the early days.

How much! There's no doubting the extent, as old Beatle favourites were used as a prelude to their newest, "Penny Lane", which, in the opinion of so many people, is their greatest track yet.

Absolutely no one can get over the marvellous few bars of trumpet in the middle and only one person has had guts enough to say: "What are they trying to do—outsell Herb Alpert?" Which is funny when you come to think of it . . .

Much as I like most of the songs on *Revolver*, I love all of the ones on "Pepper". There, I said it.

In 1966, the band had finally decided not to tour again – their terrifying exit from the Philippines, where they unintentionally snubbed the nation's first lady, Imelda Marcos, was the first of two key events that finally made them knock the old gigging lark on the head.

Essentially, after playing the Rizal Memorial Football Stadium in Manila, the band and its entourage were left to fend for themselves, pursued by a jolly batey mob with no security to protect them, and forced to pay back most of their earnings before being allowed to leave. On the flight out, Harrison told Tony Barrow, "The only way I'd ever go back to that place would be to drop a dirty big bomb on it." Fourteen years later, he was still describing it as "one of the nastiest times I have had."

The following month, on the eve of their short North American tour, they flew into a storm over Lennon's 'more popular than Jesus' comment. Some US radio stations banned the group's music, the Ku Klux Klan picketed their gigs, conservative groups staged public burnings of their records and the Vatican publicly denounced Lennon's comments.

Lennon was forced to apologise, though he would say afterwards, "I never wanted to retract a frigging word. It was all true. I was just saying how crazy it was that the Beatles had become more popular than Jesus. But then this massive row kicked off and they kept accusing me of blasphemy. To be honest, I never gave a shit what they accused me of, but I imagined some religious nutter would take a shot at one of us and that would be all down to me. I didn't want that, so I went through with saying sorry."

This was the second significant happening that convinced them not to tour again. Years later, Lennon wrote, "I always remember to thank Jesus for the end of my touring days; if I hadn't said that the Beatles were 'bigger than Jesus' and upset the very Christian Ku Klux Klan, well, Lord, I might still be up there with all the other performing fleas! God bless America. Thank you, Jesus".

So the Beatles wanted to record an album that would effectively be a show, and do the touring for them. McCartney came up with the concept of creating the fictitious Sgt. Pepper's band but, as Lennon later noted, many of the songs ultimately included could have appeared "on any other album". Nevertheless, they do comprise a series of songs thematically linked to childhood and everyday life, and the album is widely regarded as the first rock concept album. And, for the first time, none of the album's tracks appeared on singles or EPs – at least, not until many years later.

"Sgt. Pepper" opens with the sounds of a crowd (recorded in the early 60s by Martin, during a live recording of the stage show *Beyond The Fringe* - a revue written and performed by Peter Cook, Dudley Moore, Alan Bennett, and Jonathan Miller) and the Lonely Hearts Club Band tuning up (taken from the orchestra session for the final track, 'A Day in the Life'). Then the Beatles strike up and introduce the fictional band. This rockin' little titular number is reprised near the end of the album, adding further weight to the conceptual argument, but here it segues into a song sung blue by bandleader Billy Shears – a character 'played' by Starr.

'With A Little Help From My Friends' was specifically written for Starr by Lennon and McCartney, and takes the form of a Q&A session, with Starr/Shears responding to the band's enquiries. It was recorded on the day before the album's iconic artwork was shot.

Pop artist Peter Blake is generally credited for the oft-imitated sleeve art, though he was ably assisted by his then wife, Jann Haworth, art dealer Robert Fraser, and photographer Michael Cooper. The famous front cover is a colourful collage of cardboard cut-outs of famous folk (including Stu Sutcliffe), with a bunch of (cough) pot plants, and the famous Beatles themselves dressed as the Sgt. Pepper band in day-glo military outfits. The back cover shows all of the words to all of the songs, some of which were obviously influenced by the band's recreational drug use.

It's important to note here that before 1971, the UK had a relatively liberal drugs policy and the old Lysergic acid ('LSD' to you, guvnor) was still to be made a controlled substance. Nevertheless, that the Beatles were indulging was frowned upon and caused some of the tracks to be banned by the *BBC*. The situation couldn't have been helped by the fact that each of the band - and manager Epstein – put their names to an advertisement that appeared in The Times calling for the legalisation of marijuana on 24 July 1967. One of the tracks banned by the *BBC* was Lennon's psychedelic opus, 'Lucy In The Sky With Diamonds'. Lennon claimed that the inspiration for this title came from his son, Julian, who brought home from nursery school a drawing he'd done of his friend Lucy O'Donnell. Yeah, right! And that Jimi Hendrix wrote and recorded 'The Stars That Play with Laughing Sam's Dice' mere months after "Sgt. Pepper's" release is also coincidental. Pah!

The song has Harrison playing a tambura (a long-necked fretless drone lute) and McCartney on a *Lowrey* organ, both of which greatly enhance the songs dreamy feel.
"It's getting better..." was a phrase drummer Jimmie Nicol used during his brief stint with the band in the summer of 1964, after Starr collapsed and was hospitalised with tonsillitis. Although Harrison was initially against having Starr replaced, Nicol played with the band on six occasions – in Denmark, Holland, Hong Kong and Australia. After the Beatles, Nicol was called upon to stand in for Dave Clark when he became ill during a Dave Clark Five season in Blackpool. Possibly no one noticed, as Clark was neither the band's lead vocalist nor did he actually play on many of their hit singles; session drummer Bobby Graham fulfilled that function. Trivia fans will wish to note that Graham was first to be approached by Epstein when Pete Best was booted out of the Beatles; he turned down the offer as he was playing with the (then) more successful Joe Brown And The Bruvvers.

After his brief tenure with the DC5, Nicol went back to the relative obscurity from which he was plucked by producer Martin and was declared bankrupt in 1965. Many years later, his son Howie would work on the *Anthology* documentary as a sound engineer. How's that for conceptual continuity?

Now, where was I? Oh yes, McCartney utilised Nicol's phrase in the schizophrenically upbeat 'Getting Better', with help from Lennon (who contributed the more scornful lines). This song also features Harrison on tambura. During one of the sessions for the song, Lennon became disorientated having accidentally taken LSD, and was taken up to the roof of Abbey Road by Martin. Realising the potentially perilous consequences of this, McCartney and Harrison quickly brought Lennon back down. Literally.

One of the sessions for 'Fixing A Hole' took place at Regent Sound Studio – the first time the band recorded outside of Abbey Road for an album for *EMI*. The song is another ode to marijuana, whose whimsical lyrics also refer to the Beatles' fans that used to hang around outside McCartney's London home in Cavendish Avenue, and is just about the only track on the album that features anything like a discernible Harrison guitar solo.

Unusually, rather than wait for producer Martin to arrange the orchestration for 'She's Leaving Home', McCartney recruited Mike Leander, who orchestrated 'The Days Of Pearly Spencer' for David McWilliams that same year. Leander, who is perhaps best known for his work with Paul Raven (aka Gary Glitter), passed away a year before Glitter's arrest following the discovery of pornographic images of children on his laptop in 1996.

This was the only time the band consented to having one of their songs arranged by someone other than Martin, who was a little hurt but nevertheless produced 'She's Leaving Home' and conducted the string section.

The song tells the tale of a runaway girl, based on the true story of 17 year old Melanie Coe, which Lennon and McCartney read about on the front page of the *Daily Mirror*.

The lyrics to 'Being For The Benefit Of Mr. Kite!' were totally 'inspired' - 'plagiarised' might be more apt - by a 19th century circus poster for Pablo Fanque's Circus Royal, Rochdale, Lennon bought in an antique shop while filming the promotional film for 'Strawberry Fields Forever' in Sevenoaks, Kent. Multiple recordings of fairground organs and calliope music were spliced together using a William S Burroughs' style cut-up technique to create the song's middle eight. Most of the band and their roadies also played various harmonicas to add to the song's carnival atmosphere.

Harrison said, "'Within You Without You' was written after I had got into meditation... at Klaus Voormann's house in Hampstead one night after dinner." A further attempt at classical Indian music composed on a pedal harmonium, but performed on the album by Harrison with musicians from Finchley's Asian Music Circle, and none of the other Beatles (if you don't count Neil Aspinall, who played one of three tambouras). According to Hunter Davies, the band's sole official biographer, Harrison "trained himself to write down his song in Indian script so that the Indian musicians can play them."

Harrison had been taking lessons from legendary sitarist, Ravi Shankar, and had now improved significantly since his first forays with the instrument on 'Norwegian Wood'. 'Within You Without You' essentially picks up where *Revolver's* 'Love You To' left off, and was Harrison's sole tune on the album. Lennon described it as "one of George's best songs. He's clear on that song. His mind and his music are clear. There is his innate talent; he brought that sound together."

'When I'm Sixty-Four' was written by the 16 year old McCartney back in the band's Cavern days, and performed whenever the amplifiers played up. Recorded in 1966 – the year McCartney's father turned 64 – it was at one time considered as a possible b-side to either 'Strawberry Fields Forever' or 'Penny Lane' and, despite its tweeness (or perhaps because of it), is these days something of a 'standard' – a song that like 'She's Leaving Home' was either played or analysed at secondary schools in the 70s.

On McCartney's 64th birthday, his children presented him with a special version of the song, which they'd recorded at Abbey Road with the help of George Martin's son, Giles.

'Lovely Rita' is, on face if it, a straight little pop song – certainly one of the most instantly catchy here. But closer inspection reveals a veritable cornucopia of enhancements, such as the backing vocals, the playing of comb and tissue-paper, and McCartney's bass notes that all seem to float in then fade away at different times. Plus of course there's the nifty piano solo from the ever-inventive Martin. They'd utilised Martin's tinkling before (albeit mainly on album tracks), and this was a prime example of the originality that really set them apart from their contemporaries.

The lyrics to 'Good Morning Good Morning' came to Lennon after watching a television advert for that premier of 'sunshine' breakfast cereals, *Kellogg's* cornflakes – you know, the one with the big green rooster on the box. They're as English as tuppence, bold flag-bearer – even if they were invented in the US. And Cornelius Rooster can be heard at the start of this track. Seen? The song includes the sound of animals, arranged old-lady-who-swallowed-a-fly-stylee so that each one heard is capable of besting the one before it. The saxophonists from the band Sounds Incorporated (who opened the Beatles'

Shea Stadium gig) were brought in to beef-up the "fairly straight rock and roll" backing track.

After the even rockier 'Sgt. Pepper's Lonely Hearts Club Band (Reprise)' comes perhaps the albums true highlight - and one that marries two songs independently penned by Lennon and McCartney. 'A Day In The Life' starts and finishes with verses Lennon says were inspired by two stories he'd read in the *Daily Mail* (Lennon was a regular reader of the newspaper then). "One was about the Guinness heir who killed himself in a car. That was the main headline story. He died in London in a car crash. On the next page was a story about four thousand potholes in the streets of Blackburn, Lancashire, that needed to be filled. Paul's contribution was the beautiful little lick in the song, 'I'd love to turn you on,' that he'd had floating around in his head and couldn't use. I thought it was a damn good piece of work."

McCartney's middle section was, he says, "me remembering what it was like to run up the road to catch a bus to school, having a smoke and going into class. It was a reflection of my schooldays."

As ever, the producer's contribution should not be underestimated. The orchestral parts of the song were recorded using a 40-piece orchestra (which coincidentally included Alan Civil, the French horn soloist from 'For No One'), under the auspices of Martin and McCartney. Martin explained that he "wrote the lowest possible note for each of the instruments in the orchestra. At the end of the twenty-four bars, I wrote the highest note... near a chord of E major. Then I put a squiggly line right through the twenty-four bars, with reference points to tell them roughly what note they should have reached during each bar. Of course, they all looked at me as though I were completely mad."
And so the song builds to a mighty orchestral crescendo, and ends with a never-ending E-major chord played simultaneously on three pianos and a harmonium. (Well, according to Martin, it lasts for all of 42 seconds.)

But that's not all. The final track isn't listed: it appears on the run-out groove, and only ended originally when the stylus automatically lifted off the record (although that never would happen on a *Dansette* – see my comments above regarding 'Strawberry Fields Forever'). It comprises a 15-kilohertz high-frequency tone, inaudible to the human ear (which is what I am equipped with), and was included on the album at Lennon's suggestion "to annoy your dog". This is followed by a loop of gibberish and laughter from The Beatles, with the phrase "It really couldn't be any other" audible which, when played backwards, sounds nothing like "We're gonna fuck you up, sweet Satan".

I said I wouldn't dwell on the differences between the mono and stereo versions of their records, and I won't. But I heard the mono version of "Sgt. Pepper" before buying the stereo, and noticed a few variations (like different laughter at the end of 'Within You Without You'). But nothing to write home about. See, that wasn't dwelling.

However you listen to it, "Sgt. Pepper" is truly a very special album.

ALL YOU NEED IS LOVE / BABY, YOU'RE A RICH MAN

UK Release: Parlophone R 5620, 7 July 1967 (SP)
US Release: Capitol 5964, 17 July 1967 (SP)
Recording data: 14 and 25 June 1967, Olympic and EMI studios, London
Producer: George Martin
Engineer: Eddie Kramer, Geoff Emerick, Ken Scott

"This is an inspired song, because they wrote it for a worldwide programme and they really wanted to give the world a message. It could hardly have been a better message. It is a wonderful, beautiful, spine-chilling record." **– Brian Epstein**

"It was for love and bloody peace. It was a fabulous time. I even get excited now when I realise that's what it was for: peace and love, people putting flowers in guns." **– Ringo Starr**

The song introduced by Elvis Costello at Live Aid as an "old northern English folk song", starts with La Marseillaise, the national anthem of France, included according to Starr as the band's contribution to getting into the Common Market – which finally happened in 1973.

The good old *BBC* actually commissioned this song for a projected live global television broadcast, and the Beatles seized this opportunity to put across a simple message that the world could understand. Given that they would shortly be writing songs about revolution, warm guns and serial killers, we should be thankful for that.

Prior to the live broadcast (which was watched by an estimated 400 million in 26 countries), the band had put together a rhythm track consisting of piano, harpsichord, drums, and backing vocals. For the taping, they were accompanied by a small orchestra as well as many friends - including Mick Jagger, Keith Richards, Keith Moon and Graham Nash - who provided handclaps and backing vocals. Lennon was unhappy with his live vocal performance, and re-recorded his solo verses for use on the single. Starr also overdubbed drums, but Harrison left his guitar solo, which I always felt was incomplete; it certainly seems to end abruptly.

'Baby, You're A Rich Man' was the first song specially written and recorded by the band for the upcoming *United Artists'* animated film inspired by the song 'Yellow Submarine'. It features Lennon on a *Clavioline* keyboard (making the opening pipe-like sound), Mick Jagger on backing vocals, and fellow Rolling Stone and multi-instrumentalist Brian Jones on oboe.

American hip-hop trio The Fat Boys later recorded a version of 'Baby, You're A Rich Man' for the film Disorderlies, which featured a guitar solo by Frank Zappa's son, Dweezil. I mention this purely because I interviewed Dweezil in 1991, and he told me that he hadn't heard the recording since he played on it, adding "I remember that was the shortest session I ever did. I remember just playing one thing, and once I got to a certain point on the neck, I got confused as to what key I was in because it wasn't standard tuning. I started doing really weird stuff. And they kept it. That was it. Just one take of the solo. And they said. 'Great! Thanks very much.' Okay!"

For what it's worth, the song started life as 'One Of The Beautiful People'.

HELLO, GOODBYE / I AM THE WALRUS

UK Release: Parlophone R 5655, 24 November 1967 (SP)
US Release: Capitol 2056, 27 November 1967 (SP)
Recording data: 5 September & 2 October– 2 November 1967, EMI Studios, London
Producer: George Martin
Engineer: Ken Scott

"There are Geminian influences here I think: the twins. It's such a deep theme in the universe, duality - man woman, black white, ebony ivory, high low, right wrong, up down, hello goodbye - that it was a very easy song to write." – **Paul McCartney**

The words for 'I Am The Walrus' were in part inspired by Lewis Carroll's book, *Through The Looking-Glass, And What Alice Found There* – specifically, the long poem The Walrus And The Carpenter. Legend has it that "goo goo goo joob" was liberated from James Joyce's Finnegans Wake, which is total foo-ee.

McCartney's lyrics to 'Hello, Goodbye' were allegedly inspired, in part, by Alistair Taylor. During an evening at McCartney's London home - just around the corner from Abbey Road - Taylor asked him how he came up with ideas for his songs. To demonstrate how easy it was, McCartney frog-marched Taylor to his harmonium and instructed him to, "hit any note you like on the keyboard. Just hit it and I'll do the same. Now whenever I shout out a word, you shout the opposite and I'll make up a tune." And so this song opens with "You say yes, I say no. You say stop and I say go go go, oh no. You say goodbye and I say hello..."

RINGO IN FILM

BEATLE Ringo Starr will start work on his role in the new Hollywood film, Candy, some time before Christmas.

Ringo will have a "cameo role" in the film along with such stars as Richard Burton and Marlon Brando. He plays a Mexican gardener. The film will be shot in Hollywood and on location in Europe.

The Beatles have yet to fix a date for their Indian trip, but if they go in November, Ringo will have to cut his visit short in order to make the film.

Possibly because his song was relegated to the b-side, Lennon described 'Hello, Goodbye' as "three minutes of contradictions and meaningless juxtapositions", but it's a nice snappy little tune. And clever though the lyrics to 'I Am The Walrus' undoubtedly are, are they any more meaningful?

"Hela, Heba-Helloa," as some might say.

MAGICAL MYSTERY TOUR

UK Release: Parlophone MMT-1 (mono) / SMMT-1 (stereo), 8 December 1967 (EP)
US Release: Capitol MAL-2835 (mono) / SMAL-2835 (stereo), 27 November 1967 (LP)
Recording data: 25 April – 7 November 1967, EMI and Olympic Studios, London
Producer: George Martin
Engineer: Geoff Emerick, Ken Scott
Tracks: Magical Mystery Tour / Your Mother Should Know / I Am The Walrus / The Fool On The Hill / Flying / Blue Jay Way.
Additional tracks on LP version: Hello, Goodbye / Strawberry Fields Forever / Penny Lane / Baby, You're A Rich Man / All You Need Is Love

---

"You have success with something that might have seemed like a far out idea, people had said. Wow this is great. So when we'd come back again George [Martin] would be really quite keen to try, What other ideas have you got?" – **George Harrison**

Once again, the US got some new songs ahead of the UK - from the soundtrack to their 1967 'Christmas film'. These included the first song credited to all four of the band, an instrumental named 'Flying'. *Magical Mystery Tour* was the Beatles first major project following the death of manager Epstein (who died of an accidental drug overdose in August 1967, one month before homosexual activity was decriminalised in England and Wales). It is no coincidence that three of the six new songs recorded for the film were primarily penned by McCartney, though Lennon's 'I Am The Walrus' is arguably one of the band's finest moments.

After Epstein's death, it would have been very easy for McCartney to say, "Okay, that's it - the jig is up." Lennon would have quite happily sloped off into a drug-induced haze. Probably Harrison too would have been content to go it alone, as it would have enabled him to get more of his songs heard, and his new found interest in Eastern religion meant he suddenly had a surfeit of ideas to get off his chest. With Starr feeling more and more out of the loop - not being part of the band's creative core, and having just made a film away from the others with Hollywood big-hitters Marlon Brando, John Huston, James Coburn and Richard Burton - it naturally fell to McCartney to ensure that the dream wasn't over just yet.

Imagine if he had just let it slip away? While the next few years were a turbulent time for the boys, the music they produced during this period was without peer. They were already firmly established as the best group in the world, and in 1968 they were about to start crafting some of their best ever songs. Had they not all agreed to hang in there with McCartney at the helm, it's unlikely they would have come close to achieving what they then did. Their story may have had a happier ending, but the world would have been a far poorer place for it.

Musically, *Magical Mystery Tour* was a success. But the made-for-television film these songs appeared in was poorly received. Aired in the UK on Boxing Day, and in black and white, the critics slammed its vague storyline and psychedelic tomfoolery. Even the group's musical director Martin had to confess, "It looked awful and was a disaster."

I myself didn't see it until the mid-70s, in glorious living colour in a Soho cinema. After all the criticism at the time, I didn't think it was too ghastly, though some of the 'acting' (Starr and his on-screen mother, Jessie Robins) was decidedly crap - clearly ad libbed. But any film that features 'I Am The Walrus' can't be that bad. I bought it on VHS in 1989, and have always regarded it as a harmless bit of fun - like a promotional video with some Goon Show-like inserts. Victor Spinetti (making it a hat-trick of appearances in the band's movies) is great, and the Bonzo Dog Band's segment in a seedy Soho strip club is also a gas. As it lasts just under sixty minutes, I can't see that it's a waste of anyone's time.

Having now watched 2012's restored version, it looks much better and I actually wanted more - which you do get with the DVD/Blu-Ray: all the deleted scenes an' that. It stands up far better than some other rock films, that's for sure (Zappa's *200 Motels*, for example)!

Between the US and UK releases, Dr Christiaan Barnard performed the first successful human heart transplant in South Africa, prolonging Louis Washkansky's life for 18 more days. (Sadly, pneumonia put paid to Washkansky's chances of seeing the *Magical Mystery Tour* film.)

The soundtrack's new songs were initially released in the UK on a double EP, and then in long-playing format on 19 November 1976. The album version now forms part of the band's core catalogue.

CHRISTMAS TIME IS HERE AGAIN!

UK Release: Lyntone LYN 1360, 15 December 1967 (SP)
Recording data: 28 November 1967, EMI Studios, London
Producer: George Martin

An even more elaborate confection for the winter of love, and markedly a move away from Barrow's original intent for these discs. The lads had worked out a script just before recording. Its recurring 'theme' song features Lennon on two (overcoat) muffled tympani drums and Martin and Victor Spinetti helping out on backing vocals. With a storyline of folk auditioning for a *BBC* radio show, it was certainly better constructed and more professional than their other Yuletide offerings.

As on previous outings, Lennon gets to read us a poem - this time his McGonagallesque 'When Christmas Time Is Over', which was added after the others had gone home (save for Martin, who plays 'Auld Lang Syne' on the organ behind him).

The disc came in a fancy sleeve designed by Lennon, his son Julian, and Starr. But yet again, American fans were mugged off with a postcard.

LADY MADONNA / THE INNER LIGHT

UK Release: Parlophone R 5675, 15 March 1968 (SP)
US Release: Capitol 2138, 15 March 1968 (SP)
Recording data: 12 January and 3, 6 & 8 February 1968, EMI Studios, Bombay, India and London.
Producer: George Martin
Engineers: Ken Scott, Geoff Emerick

"It sounds like Elvis, doesn't it? No, it doesn't sound like Elvis. It is Elvis. Even those bits where he goes very high." – **Ringo Starr**

The first Beatles single to include a Harrison composition was also the group's last ever UK release on the *Parlophone* label (excepting posthumous reissues, obviously).

With the band's focus now shifting towards long players, McCartney proved he hadn't lost his knack of knocking out a two-minute wonder with this "bluesy boogie-woogie thing". 'Lady Madonna' references Lennon's 'I Am The Walrus' ("see how they run") and is McCartney's tribute to ordinary working class women.

The instrumental track for Harrison's b-side, 'The Inner Light', was recorded in Bombay during the sessions for his *Wonderwall Music* - the first official solo album by any of the Fab four. (While McCartney had composed the score for the film *The Family Way* in 1966, the soundtrack album – released in 1967 – was credited to The George Martin Orchestra.)

Paul may take 'tour' to States

HEARD on good authority this week we can expect a visit to New York from Paul McCartney this June. Unfortunately he will not be here to discuss another American tour, but to attend a private screening of the Beatles' "Magical Mystery Tour," which still hasn't been shown on any networks in the U.S.

The screening would be a purely private thing, Paul inviting only **Bob Dylan** and the **Young Rascals**, and hosting a party at the same time.

HEY JUDE / REVOLUTION

UK Release: Apple R 5722, 26 August 1968 (SP)
US Release: Apple 2276, 26 August 1968 (SP)
Recording data: 9–13 and 31 July 1968, EMI and Trident Studios, London
Producer: George Martin
Engineer: Ken Scott, Barry Sheffield, Geoff Emerick

"I always heard it as a song to me. If you think about it, Yoko's just come into the picture. He's saying, 'Hey, Jude - hey, John.' I know I'm sounding like one of those fans who reads things into it, but you can hear it as a song to me. The words 'go out and get her' - subconsciously he was saying, go ahead, leave me. On a conscious level, he didn't want me to go ahead. The angel in him was saying, 'Bless you.' The devil in him didn't like it at all because he didn't want to lose his partner." **– John Lennon**

Their longest ever single (at seven minutes 11 seconds), 'Hey Jude' was the first record to be released on the band's own *Apple* label and the first song they recorded at Trident studios – making use of the eight-track facilities there. Peter Asher, the head of A&R at *Apple* and brother of McCartney's then fiancée Jane, was working with the label's new signing James Taylor at Trident when McCartney paid them a visit. It was there and then that McCartney decided it was the right place to record his new composition.

Despite the quote above, it is generally accepted that McCartney originally wrote this for Lennon's son Julian ("Hey Jules") during a drive down to their home in Weybridge to comfort the then five year old and his distraught mother, Cynthia – Lennon having left them to be with Ono. Cynthia later wrote, "I will never forget Paul's gesture of care and concern in coming to see us. It made me feel important and loved, as opposed to feeling discarded and obsolete. Paul gave me a great deal of strength and hope."

Rather ironically, Jane Asher was to end her relationship with McCartney a couple of weeks before the recording of Hey Jude having discovered him in bed with American scriptwriter, Francie Schwartz. Funny how the band never seemed to settle down with nice English girls, isn't it? Both Starr and Harrison divorced their first wives in the mid-70s and married, respectively, American and Mexican ladies.

McCartney slightly altered the lyrics to make them less specific (claiming that the name Jude was "a bit more country and western"), and told Lennon he would 'fix' the nonsensical line "the movement you need is on your shoulder." Lennon urged him not to, arguing it was the strongest line in the song and he knew just what it meant.

On the recording, the bit where Lennon joins McCartney on the last verse (before the lengthy four-chord 'nah nah nah' coda) always sends a shiver up my spine. But I didn't realise he sang "into" instead of "under" and that his "Oh! Fucking hell!" expletive can be heard. Headphones on, kiddiwinks.

The song was phenomenally successful, boosted by a promotional film shot at Twickenham Film Studios by Michael Lindsay-Hogg that was broadcast in the US (on The Smothers Brothers Comedy Hour) and UK (on The David Frost Show, where the host introduced them as "the greatest tea-room orchestra in the world"). The film was recorded on 4 September, and marked the return of Starr, who had quit the band two weeks previously.

Starr had walked out on 22 August, the very day that Cynthia sued Lennon for divorce on the grounds of adultery, and McCartney had begun work on the first track of their next album

Although the band joked about Starr's talents as a drummer, in reality they all appreciated his reliability and good humour, and were genuinely devastated when he walked out. Starr said, "I left because I felt two things: I felt I wasn't playing great, and I also felt the other three were really happy and I was an outsider." They persuaded him to return and, as a welcome back gesture, they had Mal Evans put flowers all around his drum kit before he arrived back in the studio.

'Hey Jude' was the biggest ever debut release for a record label, selling an estimated eight million copies worldwide and topping the charts in eleven countries. No mean feat. So why do some people loathe and detest it so much? Difficult to say, but it might be McCartney's hokey "You were great!" embellishments he has often inappropriately applied to its anthemic ending during subsequent post-Fab live outings. Either that or they've just got no taste, as you really can't fault the original.

Prior to recording the song, McCartney gave a unique solo performance of it on Sunday 30 June at the Oakley Arms in the village of Harrold in Bedfordshire. McCartney showed up out of the blue and performed on the pub's piano. It is no surprise that it has become one of the most talked about events in the village's history. John Keech: "It had been just another weekend. Sunday night came around too soon as usual. I settled down to watch the telly when I realised I was out of cigarettes. It must have been about 8.30pm when I walked into the pub. When I got into the bar I bumped into a gentleman who turned out to be a chauffeur. He told me I should go through to the Lounge. Looking around everything looked the same, the same décor, the piano standing by the fireplace, the same crowd! Then amongst my friends I spotted a very familiar face, suddenly the place that I was in was very extraordinary. It was Paul McCartney chatting away like he had lived here all his life. It was like a dream but the distinctive lilt to his voice was unmistakeable."

"Apparently he was on his way back to London from Leeds accompanied by Peter Asher. In order to break the journey, they were in the habit of getting a map and sticking a pin in it and then going to the place where the pin landed. That night the pin hit Harrold."

"When I got a chance to talk to Paul I told him that we had been born in the same hospital, I am just 2 months older than him! With that he told me to come over to the piano and sit beside him, while he played a few of his songs. He then announced that he was just finishing a new song and would like to play it for the first time in public for us. The song was 'Hey Jude'. The inevitable autograph had to be dedicated to my daughter Judith (Jude), written on the only paper I had available – a ten-shilling note."

"The ending – I went home to tell Jen what had just happened. I had popped out for a packet of cigarettes at 8.30pm, by this time it was midnight. I will leave you to imagine the reaction when I told her that I had been delayed because I had met Paul McCartney!"

A somewhat different account from Tony Bramwell, who had accompanied Paul McCartney and entourage, including Paul's Old English Sheepdog, Martha, en route from the north of England wrote a few years later: "On a Sunday afternoon in June 1968... we set off back to London. Getting bored with non-stop M1, Paul suggested we pull out the *AA* book and find a village with the nicest name... and pop off the motorway for a change of scenery. After a short time Harrold in Bedfordshire was spotted... and a detour was made. On entering this pretty little village, we spotted a gent who was trimming his hedge and he looked suspiciously at the Rolls as we drove past. We went through the village without seeing anyone on this lovely afternoon, turned round and asked the gent if there was a tearoom or pub open, but he said not. Recognising Paul, he invited us into his home to have some tea and told us that the pub would be open shortly."

"He told us that he was a dentist practising in Bedford, and he introduced his wife and children who seemed perfectly at ease that a Beatle should drop in for Sunday tea! We then went along to the pub with Paul and were greeted very warmly by the landlord and were made to feel very welcome. Pretty soon the whole village seemed to appear in the pub and it looked like things might get out of hand, so we went back to the dentist's house and opened a bottle of wine. His little girl brought out a guitar and Paul sang some of his new songs to the gathered family, including one he had just finished called 'Hey Jude'."

"We were then told that the pub had been cleared of all but the real locals and we were invited back for a quiet drink after hours. Paul was pretty swiftly sat at the piano and he played a selection of standards and Beatles' classics as the locals sang along."

"At about three o'clock in the morning we quite drunkenly climbed into the car and were then driven back to London. During the following week we sent up some records and champagne to be raffled at the Church Fete."

THE BEATLES

UK Release: Apple (Parlophone) PMC 7067-7068 (mono) / PCS 7067-7068 (stereo), 22 November 1968 (LP)
US Release: Apple (Capitol) SWBO-101, 25 November 1968 (LP)
Recording data: 30 May – 14 October 1968, EMI and Trident Studios, London.
Producer: George Martin
Engineers: Geoff Emerick, Ken Scott, Barry Sheffield, Ken Townsend
Tracks: Back In The U.S.S.R. / Dear Prudence / Glass Onion / Ob-La-Di Ob-La-Da / Wild Honey Pie / The Continuing Story Of Bungalow Bill / While My Guitar Gently Weeps / Happiness Is A Warm Gun / Martha My Dear / I'm So Tired / Blackbird / Piggies / Rocky Raccoon / Don't Pass Me By / Why Don't We Do It In The Road? / I Will / Julia / Birthday / Yer Blues / Mother Nature's Son / Everybody Got Something To Hide Except Me And My Monkey / Sexy Sadie / Helter Skelter / Long, Long, Long / Revolution 1 / Honey Pie / Savoy Truffle / Cry Baby Cry / Revolution 9 / Good Night

---

"Sgt. Pepper did its thing, it was the album of the decade - of the century maybe. It was very innovative, great songs, glad I was on it. But The White Album, we ended up being more of a band again and that's what I always love; I love being in a band." – **Ringo Starr**

Lennon had wanted to call the next album *A Doll's House*, after the book by Norwegian writer Henrik Ibsen. But that title was dropped when Leicester band Family's debut album, *Music In A Doll's House*, was released in July 1968.

Born in India, 'The White Album' (as it is popularly known) is a bit of a hotchpotch – the lads themselves were apparently not too enamoured of it on its release. But for my money, this is the best Beatles album ever – largely because there's so much on it, but also because it sees the band unfettered, just being themselves. The real Beatles, if you like. Rampant.

Having said that – and noting Starr's comment above – I should point out here that only 16 of the album's 30 tracks actually feature all four Beatles. Yes, the cracks were showing. The clocks were baring their teeth. Listen to the loonies croon. I love it!

Although I have been buying records for most of my life and have a pretty extensive library of tunes, I am by no means a rabid collector. But *The Beatles* is the one album I have in three different formats: on vinyl, music-cassette and compact disc. Twice.

After the care and attention lavished on "Sgt. Pepper", the band – Lennon and McCartney, in particular - had proven to the world they were capable of honing and harnessing the skills learnt in their earlier touring years to produce a great, succinct work of art in the studio. Now they were free to do as they pleased.

The Beatles is a double album that you really can't whittle down to one disc (as was producer Martin's desire). No way. And even if you did half its length, it would still have been their longest album to date. But which babies would you murder? Imagine if they hadn't included 'Revolution 9' (which McCartney actually wanted). It would be more sought after than the still unreleased 'Carnival Of Light' (which Harrison vetoed for inclusion on *Anthology 2*). It was a bold thing to release at the time, and that's yet another example of what makes the Beatles such a groundbreaking band. And anyway, there exists many longer versions of the songs here, so they self-edited anyway. Just love it and leave it out, alright?

As noted above, it was while recording the album's first track that Starr walked out on the band for two weeks. McCartney had a hissy fit when Starr fucked up a fill, and ended up playing the drums himself on a song he'd been inspired to write as a tongue in cheek parody of Chuck Berry's 'Back In The USA'.

'Back In The U.S.S.R.' was written in Rishikesh - the world capital of Yoga - where the band had gone to stay and meditate at the Maharishi Mahesh Yogi's ashram. It was here that they learned of the passing of Epstein and were inspired to write the bulk of the tracks that ended up on the album.

Before recording proper began, the Beatles assembled at Kinfauns, Harrison's home in Esher, where they took the unusual step of demoing 27 of their new songs – something they hadn't ever done before. Seven of these demos ended up on *Anthology 3*, while the others have appeared on various bootlegs. It has been suggested that an album called Primal Colours comprising some of these *Ampex* 4-track home recordings, together with early studio sessions for "The White Album", was mooted at the time. But it seems highly unlikely that the whole band would have sanctioned such a ramshackle collection, bootlegs of which start with the unfunny Brian Epstein Blues, a pretty dreadful song seemingly improvised during the recording of 'Sexy Sadie'.

Mike Love of the Beach Boys was also staying at Rishikesh, which prompted McCartney to lyrically lampoon 'California Girls', the hit Love had penned with fellow Beach Boy Brian Wilson a few years earlier. For good measure, he also incorporated some Beach Boy-like harmonies into his commie-loving anthem. The song opens/closes with the sound of a Vickers Viscount jet plane taking off/landing, and is a thrustingly good opening track.

The introduction to Lennon's 'Dear Prudence' plays over the sound of the jet fading away. This song has always been a favourite of mine, and I'll never forgive Siouxsie And The Banshees for the awful cover version they inflicted upon the world in 1983. Yes, it might've given them their biggest ever hit and temporarily revived their already flagging career (their only subsequent top 20 single was another cover: Dylan's 'This Wheel's On Fire'), but it sullies one of the greatest, unfussy songs of all time. Its composer, his son Julian and Jerry Garcia of the Grateful Dead all share my view of the original's potent simplicity.

And according to Morrissey (in his autobiography), Siouxsie is "a physical blancmange that is six parts Kate O'Mara, two parts Myra Hindley and two parts Fenella Fielding." So there.

'Dear Prudence' utilises a finger-picking style that Donovan - 'the Scottish Dylan' - had taught Lennon and Harrison while in India. Its lyrics relate to Prudence Farrow, the sister of actress Mia. Both the Farrow girls were also out in Rishikesh with the band in early 1968.

In June that year, the film *Rosemary's Baby* was released. Written and directed by Roman Polanski, he'd originally wanted his wife Sharon Tate to play the part of Rosemary but relented and agreed to cast the more marketable Mia (who starred in the popular US soap opera, Peyton Place - and had also just separated from her husband, Frank Sinatra). Hope your taking notes here: I'll get back to some of this in a mo.

Seemingly while in Rishikesh, Prudence took to the old meditation lark big time – to the extent that she had to be coaxed out of her room by Lennon to 'play'. He penned and played this for her while out there.

Prudence went on to gain a BA, an MA, and a PhD in Asian studies, and has taught Transcendental Meditation in Florida on and off since 1970. She also managed Raith Rovers during the 90s, overseeing their brief UEFA Cup run in the 1995-96 season.

'Glass Onion' is the first track on the album to feature the now placated Starr on drums. The band's spirits were further buoyed by Lennon's jokey reference to McCartney being the Walrus. The song in fact cross-references a number of older Beatles songs in a deliberate attempt to wind-up those who tried to read too much into their lyrics – Lennon's in particular.

McCartney's 'Ob-La-Di Ob-La-Da' no doubt further confused those looking for deeper meaning, though the title is said to be Yorùbá (a Niger–Congo language spoken in West Africa) for the rather simple, er, "Life goes on". McCartney picked this phrase up from Jimmy Scott, the Nigerian conga player and leader of the Obladi Oblada Band, who he met at Soho's Bag O' Nails private members club. Scott reputedly played on the recording, and later tried to screw some wedge outta Macca for liberating a phrase he claimed as his own. He succeeded, but not in a court of law. Possibly because at the time Scott was serving time in HM Prison Brixton for running up maintenance debts. According to Alistair Taylor, McCartney had him hand over £800 to Scott in Brixton – to both spring him from gaol and keep him sweet.

Sadly, Scott passed away in 1986 following a tour with Bad Manners. The band's lead singer, Buster Bloodvessel (aka Douglas Trendle: his stage name was taken from the bus conductor played by Ivor Cutler in the *Magical Mystery Tour* film), explained: "We'd just done this tour of America and he caught pneumonia. When he got back to Britain he was strip-searched at the airport because he was Nigerian. They left him naked for two hours. The next day he was taken into hospital and he died."

The piano-pounding introduction was played by a zonked-out Lennon who was growing increasingly frustrated by McCartney's attempts to perfect the piece in the studio. Like McCartney's own slip of the tongue (he mistakenly sings "Desmond stays at home and does his pretty face"), both were included in the final recording in keeping with the general laissez-faire message of the song.

Although it was an obvious candidate as a single, 'Ob-La-Di Ob-La-Da' was not released by the band on 7-inch in the UK. And so, a cover version by Marmalade went straight to number one in January 1969 instead. Marmalade though replaced the word "bra" with "whoa", the pussies. (Having said that, Marmalade were in fact pretty brave to have called themselves The Gaylords when starting out in their native Glasgow in the early 60s.) Elsewhere, the Fabs' version of 'Ob-La-Di Ob-La-Da' topped singles charts around the globe.

'Wild Honey Pie' was ad-libbed by McCartney as a very short prelude to a new song he'd just written, called 'Honey Pie'. Being a very quick solo multi-track experiment, it almost didn't make it onto the album. But Harrison's wife Pattie apparently liked it, so it stayed. And it's really the off-guard inbetweeny pieces like this – and the sound effects - that, for me, help make "The White Album" that extra bit special. Such 'musical grouting' would become quite commonplace in rock music after this album, but I wouldn't go so far as to say that the Beatles invented it – just made it popular. Whatever people might say about them, there's no denying just how incredibly influential they were.

At the same session, McCartney tried-out another work-in-progress called 'Etcetera'. This mutated into the instrumental piece 'Thingumybob', recorded a few months later by John Foster & Son Ltd Black Dyke Mills Band and produced by McCartney. This was released as part of the first batch of singles from *Apple Records*, which also included 'Hey Jude', and featured the Yorkshire brass band's version of 'Yellow Submarine' on the flip side.

Lennon's fab sing-along piece, 'The Continuing Story Of Bungalow Bill', includes the only female lead vocal on a Beatles' recording. The very brief line ("Not when he looks so fierce...") is sung by Ono, whose increased intrusion in the studio would lead to more and more disharmony in the ranks. But for the time being, she was tolerated – not least because this particular recording also featured backing vocals from Mrs Starr. Pattie Harrison and McCartney's stop-gap squeeze Francie Schwartz would similarly contribute background voices to "The White Album."

'Bungalow Bill' is a thinly veiled reference to one Richard Cooke III, an American man who joined the meditation course in Rishikesh and left briefly to shoot tigers. Lennon was inspired by this episode to pen this seemingly light-hearted song, which he himself described as "a sort of teenage social-comment". Very, very pleasant music, I calls it. The song opens with a short disparate Spanish guitar flourish that was one of the 18 seven-second instrument samples embedded in the Mellotron Mark II.

Although not listed as playing on the album, guitarist Eric Clapton was invited to play lead on Harrison's 'While My Guitar Gently Weeps'. Clapton at that time was in rock supergroup Cream, who were on the verge of disbanding and preparing songs for their final album and farewell tour. Clapton was taken aback - though very flattered - to be asked to appear on a Beatles' record, even though he wasn't especially fond of their music.

In his autobiography, he talks of his hatred for Beatlemania and all it stood for, and of the time the Beatles went to see the Rolling Stones at the Crawdaddy club, and he decided they were "a bunch of wankers." But he did quickly bond with Harrison, and by this time was happy to do his bidding. It is generally felt that Clapton's presence in the studio also relieved some of the tension that was building between band members.

His solo was played on Harrison's Gibson Les Paul (a gift from Clapton), and recorded in one take. Clapton would then invite Harrison to help with a song for Cream's Goodbye album, to which Starr also made a small-uncredited contribution (even though, as Harrison states in his book I Me Mine, he was "absolutely plastered"). That song that would eventually be named 'Badge', with Harrison playing rhythm guitar in the guise of L'Angelo Misterioso (he would though receive a co-writing credit with Clapton under his real name).

Several weeks after the sessions for 'While My Guitar Gently Weeps', Harrison dropped off copies of the acetates for "The White Album" at Clapton's abode. On Cream's last tour of the US, Clapton played the album to all and sundry, thinking he was doing his new pal a favour by presenting this music to a more discerning audience. When he found out, Harrison evidently blew his top and gave Clapton a real bollocking. But the incident did no long-term damage to their friendship, which would also endure the divorce of Harrison from Pattie and her eventual marriage to Clapton.

Producer Martin had showed Lennon the cover of a gun magazine (The American Rifleman) sporting the headline 'Happiness Is a Warm Gun'. Lennon thought it "a fantastic, insane thing to say. A warm gun means you just shot something!" His song of that name was comprised of sections from four different songs he was working on at the time. Consequently, the piece features a number of changes in both key and time signature that saw McCartney and Harrison working closely with the song's composer to get it just so. The pair subsequently agreed it was the best song on the album. Lyrically it's by turns surreal, hilarious and uniquely British. And also largely influenced by sex and drugs and Derek Taylor.

It's debatable whether 'Martha My Dear' is really about McCartney's ex-wife-to-be, Asher, or his pet Old English Sheepdog, Martha. McCartney claims the latter, but the "don't forget me" line implies the former. Where the preceding track was very much a band effort (as well as originally being the last track on side one), 'Martha My Dear' featured only the one Beatle - on vocals, piano, bass, lead guitar, drums and handclaps. Martin wrote the brass and string arrangement, based on McCartney's earlier demo.

'I'm So Tired' is another song inspired by Lennon's much-loved pastime. Penned in Rishikesh, where a restless Lennon was pining for Ono. Cynthia had thought she and Lennon might "rediscover our lost closeness" while away from the usual distractions of drink and drugs, but it seems the opposite was true; after a fortnight away, her old man upped and moved to a separate room.

Lennon said 'I'm So Tired' ended up being one of his favourite songs – "I like the sound of it, and I sing it well." It contains a classic line about Sir Walter Raleigh, the man who introduced tobacco to England. Like the rest of the Beatles, Lennon was a heavy smoker and he clearly couldn't relax with a Harry in his hand. The song ends with Lennon muttering "Monsieur, monsieur, monsieur, how about another one?"

And another cracker followed, sure enough. McCartney's 'Blackbird' was composed on his farm in Scotland just after the band returned from their trip to India. He performed it a little later for the fans camped outside his London home on the first night his wife to be, Linda Eastman, stayed over. McCartney says the song is an allegorical message of support to an oppressed black woman living in Little Rock ("Those were the days of the civil rights movement, which all of us cared passionately about."). He recorded it solo with just an acoustic guitar, and added some bird song effects. He later claimed his guitar playing was inspired by Bach's Bourrée, a piece he and Harrison had attempted to learn as youngsters to show off to their pals. The result is simple, but incredibly effective.

The second in the trio of animal songs (purposely sequenced that way by Messrs Lennon and McCartney) was Harrison's 'Piggies'. An unusual song from his expanding canon, with its Baroque harpsichord, strings and lyrical attack on financial greed and class conflict. The words were actually written a couple of years previous (around the same time as 'Taxman'), and tweaked for this recording. More sound effects abound (yeah, pig noises). Unfortunately, Harrison's words were misconstrued by Charles Manson, the infamous serial killer by proxy, with devastating consequences.

Manson was a nut-job convinced that black people would rise up and kill whites, but that he and his followers (or 'family') could be saved via a set of clues in "The White Album". In Manson's mind, 'Piggies' represented the doomed whites.

On 8 August 1969, Manson instructed four of his followers to go to 10050 Cielo Drive in Los Angeles to kill the occupants. The house had belonged to Doris Day's son, Terry Melcher, whom Manson had earlier befriended in a failed bid to kick-start a career in music. At that time, though, film director Roman Polanski and his actress wife, Sharon Tate, were renting the house (see I told you I'd get back to them). Manson's followers entered the house and viciously murdered Tate, her unborn child, and four others who were visiting her; Polanski was away in foggy London town working on *A Day At The Beach*. Afterwards, one of the family wrote "pig" on the house's front door in Tate's blood. Harrison's song isn't that brilliant, but it doesn't deserve to be associated with these twats.

'Rocky Raccoon' is a silly but fun folk pastiche by McCartney, memorable for the line about the girl of the eponymous character's fancy: "Her name was Magil, and she called herself Lil. But everyone knew her as Nancy." Now that's class.

'Don't Pass Me By' is Starr's first solo composition for the Beatles, which he seemingly started writing – as a country and western number – back in 1963. During two separate radio interviews the year after that, both Lennon and McCartney sang a verse and Starr was asked whether the band would actually record it. "I keep trying to push it on them every time we make a record," was his reply. His persistence eventually paid off and he and McCartney recorded it together in June/July 1968. Starr said afterwards, "It was great to get my first song down, one that I had written. It was a very exciting time for me and everyone was really helpful, and recording that crazy violinist was a thrilling moment."

The fiddle was added by jazz musician and promoter, Jack Fallon, who was surprised that they kept the sound of him "scraping away" at the song's end: "It was pretty dreadful," he thought. Well, that was his opinion. It just wouldn't be the same without it, and the way it segues into another blues structured piano-driven piece of fun by the pair (Lennon and Harrison were evidently busy supervising string overdubs for Piggies and Glass Onion that day).

'Why Don't We Do It In The Road?' was penned by McCartney after he observed a pair of monkeys nonchalantly fornicating in a street in Rishikesh, India. The Idle Race's Jeff Lynne observed McCartney recording this using a Fender Jazz bass "with the price tag hanging off!" Despite being miffed by his non-involvement in the song's recording, Lennon said he enjoyed the piece... and the ensuing royalties, no doubt.

'I Will' is a nicely understated slice of McCartney magic, somewhat overshadowed by Lennon's subsequent effort, which may have topped McCartney's song lyrically but not melodically. Although Harrison didn't feature on the recording, he did later accompany McCartney on this tune – on the ukulele – during filming of the *Anthology* documentary.

So what's so great about Lennon's lyrics for 'Julia?' First and foremost, it is a song of love for his late mother, who was killed by an inebriated off-duty police constable in a road accident on 15 July 1958. This event naturally greatly distressed the teenager, who named his firstborn after her. But it also drew him close to McCartney, who lost his mother Mary two years earlier.

The song includes the line "Julia, ocean child, calls me," which is a reference to Ono, whose name means 'child of the sea' in Japanese. (Lennon would later often spookily refer to Ono as 'mother'.)

So, 'Julia' is a real heartfelt song of some pretty mixed-up emotions and a real turning point for Lennon whose lyrics would now become more and more open and honest. Musically, it again copped the guitar technique taught him by Donovan in India. The song is also distinguished by being – in the spirit of 'anything McCartney can do, I can do equally well' - the one Beatles' recording made by Lennon where he alone accompanied himself (although, as evidenced by the version on *Anthology 3*, McCartney was in the control room keeping a watching eye on proceedings). 'Julia' was the last song to be started for "The White Album", which would be finished and on the streets less than six weeks later.

'Birthday' was one of the songs not written in India or demoed at Kinfauns, it was just "50-50 John and me, made up on the spot and recorded all in the same evening," according to McCartney. But that's probably being generous to Lennon, who (like many other Fab songs) would later dismiss this one as "garbage". It's not, but it also isn't one that gets played on people's birthdays all that often, which was McCartney's hope. It was one of the songs that featured all four of the band, though without the involvement of producer Martin, who was away on his hols. During the session, the band had all nipped round the corner to McCartney's house to watch the UK TV premiere of The Girl Can't Help It, which perhaps accounts for this rockin' rhythm record that opens side three (or the second half) of the album.

Lennon's semi-satirical 'Yer Blues' is another song played and recorded by all four members – "in a box, a room about eight by eight, with no separation," said Starr. It's surprising that this fairly basic, stripped down number was largely recorded on the same day as Lennon's avant-garde 'What's The New Mary Jane' – which was deemed too off-piste for "The White Album". Recorded with Harrison, Ono and Mal Evans, Lennon proposed to issue "Mary Jane" as the b-side of a single by the Plastic One Band, the 'conceptual supergroup' he formed with Ono the following year. But that idea too was dropped and the song remained much bootlegged and unreleased for 28 years.

The month after "The White Album" came out, Lennon performed 'Yer Blues' for The

Rolling Stones Rock and Roll Circus TV special. This was the first time since forming the Beatles that Lennon had played in public without them. Picking up on his blues-boom piss-take, he named the group The Dirty Mac after Fleetwood Mac, whose 'Albatross' single had just hit the charts heading for the number one spot. The Dirty Mac comprised Lennon, Eric Clapton, the Stones' Keith Richards and Mitch Mitchell, drummer with The Jimi Hendrix Experience.

'Mother Nature's Son' is another solo McCartney recording, which further pissed Lennon off. McCartney was motivated to write the song after a lecture by the Maharishi in India, though he believes he actually penned it at his father's house in Liverpool with the song 'Nature Boy' (as made famous by Nat King Cole) very much at the forefront of his mind. Lennon apparently helped with some of the words, though he too wrote his own song following the lecture called 'I'm Just A Child Of Nature'. Lennon demoed his song at Kinfauns, but it was not taken forward until a few years later when he re-wrote the lyrics and it became 'Jealous Guy' on his second post-Beatles solo studio album. McCartney's song provides some light relief between a batch of group-performed songs at the start of side three.

'Everybody Got Something To Hide Except Me And My Monkey' is a song written by Lennon about his relationship with Ono... and heroin. A percussion heavy rocker on which all four clapped, hit and shook things. The song was speeded up to add to its frenetic feel. Okay, so the Walrus was Paul, the monkey was Yoko and, as any fule kno, 'Sexy Sadie' was the Maharishi. While in Rishikesh, Lennon heard a rumour that the Maharishi had made a pass at one of the girls there - possibly Mia Farrow, who years later became adept at rewriting history to suit her own ends (first making out that Woody Allen was a kiddie-fiddler, then intimating that Frank Sinatra might have been the father of Allen's son, Satchel). Anyway, this was cause enough for Lennon to decide that the meditation teacher was "a little twat" and that he wanted nothing more to do with him – whereas, in truth, he was probably just looking for any excuse to fly home and be with Ono. Great song, though – one that not even the old Modfather, Paul Weller, could fuck up.

'Helter Skelter' is another song Siouxsie And The Banshees covered. Okay, I'll grudgingly admit they didn't quite ruin it. But look, she was born eight months before me and raised less than five miles from me: hell, I could've been part of the Bromley contingent and become a punk musician; clearly talent was not a requirement, but instead I chose to stay in my bedroom listening to Camel and reading Kurt Vonnegut. I also didn't think that wearing Swastikas was funny or shocking. Yeah: Nazi punks, fuck off! But that's not why I don't like Siouxsie Sioux; she's just not a great singer. Sorry.

U2's Bono presumptuously tried to reclaim 'Helter Skelter' for the Beatles after that psycho Manson named his prediction of an apocalyptic war after it. You see, two days after the Tate murders, three of Manson's family murdered Leno and Rosemary LaBianca, and one of the illiterate killers used their blood to write "Healter Skelter" on their fridge. Anyway, the Beatles' song – for it is and always will be theirs and theirs alone – was McCartney's attempt to create the loudest, rawest, dirtiest song he could.

It seems there were plenty of hi-jinks taking place in the studio during its final recording session in September, which saw them lay down 18 takes. (The band had originally recorded three slower, much longer versions in July.)

After the eighteenth take, an exasperated Starr threw his sticks across the studio and shouted, "I got blisters on me fingers!" – a phrase that was beautifully captured and included on the album.

Following the preceding whirlpool of sex and drugs and mock and roll songs, Harrison's 'Long, Long, Long' can get overlooked – tucked away at the end of side three on this monster of an album. But it really is a gem. Take it out, madam – go on, put it on your finger.

Influenced by Dylan's 'Sad Eyed Lady Of The Lowlands', this too is a love song though to God rather than his wife (hey, as noted elsewhere, Pattie got plenty of top toons written for her). Recorded sans Lennon, McCartney's Hammond organ enhances the song's haunting quality, as do Starr's drums as they roll in and out, complementing Harrison's vocals perfectly. Producer Martin explains the odd ending thusly: "There's a sound near the end of the song which is a bottle of Blue Nun wine rattling away on top of a Leslie speaker cabinet. Paul hit a certain note and the bottle started vibrating. We thought it was so good that we set the mic's up and did it again."

'Revolution 1' is an earlier, slower arrangement of the hard-rocking song that graced the backside of 'Hey Jude'. On this version, Lennon is unsure whether he's up for radical change when he sings "you can count me out... in" This version originally ran for over ten minutes, with a far more way-out coda featuring tape loops, overdubs, sped-up vocals and chanting and other spooky weirdness. Lennon eventually decided to split the song in half, with parts of the discarded part winding up in the full-on experimental 'Revolution 9'.

The not-so wild (and not at all destructive) 'Honey Pie' follows. Like 'When I'm Sixty-Four', this is a music hall kinda song much beloved of McCartney; although very much his baby, Lennon played ball by adding a very Django-ish guitar solo.

'Savoy Truffle' was inspired by God's teeth. As Harrison noted in his book I Me Mine, Eric Clapton had a lot of cavities around this time and needed dental work. "He always had toothache but he ate a lot of chocolates – he couldn't resist them and once he saw a box he had to eat them all. He was over at my house and I had a box of Good News chocolates on the table and wrote the song from the names inside the lid." Mackintosh's, the company that manufactured Good News, merged with Rowntree to form Rowntree Mackintosh in 1969; they stopped making the chocolates sometime in the mid-70s. An overdub for 'Savoy Truffle' on 14 October 1968 marked the end of recording sessions for the album.

The recording of 'Cry Baby Cry' saw another walk-out: this time engineer Geoff Emerick, who had had enough of the arguing and swearing. He got better though, and returned several months later.

'Cry Baby Cry' was yet another song that Lennon would later declare "a piece of rubbish", but we know better. With its references to the nobility (its mention of the Duchess of Kirkcaldy would come back to haunt me later in life when, for a brief moment in the noughties, I worked alongside the Member of Parliament for Kirkcaldy, Dr Lewis Moonie; a very amiable sort, I must say), séances, "voices out of nowhere" plus a far from simple drum pattern from Starr, it's better than bad it's good. The Danes call it quality. It is then followed by a short unlisted McCartney improvisation, referred to as 'Can You Take Me Back', that acts as an intro to the album's centrepiece.

'Revolution 9' can be seen either as a humongous piece of musical grouting or a groundbreaking work of art that would help open the closed minds of the youth of Britain. Yes, just five short years later, mousey-haired denim clad herberts would think nothing of shelling out 49p for a copy of *The Faust Tapes*, largely because of this track. Clearly such an experimental sound collage was not an original idea – in rock, Zappa had released a whole album of musique concrete (*Lumpy Gravy*) the year before, and Varèse and Stockhausen had been pioneering such tape experiments since the early 50s. But the Beatles had the capacity to reach far more people, and thus make something previously alien to the masses more acceptable – such as the wacky idea that 'anything can be music'.

Largely a Lennon concoction, throughout we hear the repeated phrase "number nine", which he explained was taken from "an engineer's testing voice saying, 'This is *EMI* test series number nine'. I just cut up whatever he said and I'd number ninc it. Nine turned out to be my birthday and my lucky number and everything. I didn't realise it: it was just so funny the voice saying, 'number nine'; it was like a joke, bringing number nine into it all the time, that's all it was." Lennon's first home was also number 9 Newcastle Road, and he's quite right: it does have a very humorous impact. Oh my. And being sandwiched between an unsettling nursery rhyme and a lullaby augments the overall sense of surrealism of the final part of this album.

And yes, but also. How best to now end this ever so slightly flawed masterpiece of a record? 'Good Night' ensured that all four members of the Beatles recorded a song credited to the group without the other members performing. In this instance not even its writer appears: composed by Lennon as a lullaby for his son Julian, 'Good Night' is sumptuously sung by Starr, backed by a full orchestra beautifully arranged and conducted by Martin. Again, such a contrast to what went before and confirmation that they knew not only how to please themselves, but also their fans.

And so ends an album that, as you may have noted, makes me get a little angry when people dare to try and associate themselves with it – by dissing its songs, covering them, or hijacking them with murderous intent.

With the band's unity diminishing further as the 60s drew to a close, they turned a little more to what had brought them together in the first place –straightforward rock/pop songs about peace, love and octopi. That's not to say that they didn't produce anything further of note or on subjects other than cars and girls, for they most certainly did. But after "The White Album", they would never be as experimental or daring again.

The Beatles was released five years to the day after *With The Beatles*, when Lyndon Baines Johnson was still president of the United States. As vice president, LBJ had assumed the presidency immediately after JFK's assassination, and was subsequently elected for the role in his own right in 1964. In those five years, he oversaw the march towards the Great Society - which strove to eliminate poverty and racial injustice - while over here the Beatles got high and changed the face of music. Shit, the sixties must've been great!

THE BEATLES' 1968 CHRISTMAS RECORD

UK Release: Lyntone LYN 1743/4, 20 December 1968 (SP)
Recording data: November–December 1968, various locations.
Producer: Kenny Everett

After the previous couple of well-forged efforts, this was the first Christmas fan-club flexi to be recorded by the lads individually at home, with the exception of Harrison who recorded his part at the New York apartment of attorney Nathan Weiss. As a consequence, it's is a bit of a mish-mash. It is also the longest one they ever issued. And again it reflects where their heads were at, man: in his 'Unwinese' poem Two Virgins, Lennon clearly chides the others about how over the last year he and his new love had "battled on against overwhelming oddities, includo some of their beast friends".

Elsewhere, McCartney strums an acoustic guitar and sings 'Happy Christmas, Happy New Year', Starr has a droll phone conversation with himself, and Tiny Tim is introduced by Harrison and prompted to perform 'Nowhere Man' as only he could (something the American singer/ukulele player did that year at London's Royal Albert Hall, with the accompaniment of a full-sized orchestra). Clips from "The White Album" can also be heard throughout, including 'Ob-La-Di, Ob-La-Da', 'Yer Blues', 'Birthday', and a sped-up smidge of 'Helter Skelter'. This was all hacked together by British comedian, radio DJ, television entertainer and friend of the Beatles, Kenny Everett.

US fans finally got a flexi-disc for Christmas this year, but in a modified version of the 1967 UK sleeve.

YELLOW SUBMARINE

UK Release: Apple (Parlophone) PMC 7070 (mono) / PCS 7070 (stereo), 17 January 1969 (LP)
US Release: Apple (Capitol) SW-153, 13 January 1969 (LP)
Recording data: 26 May 1966 – 11 February 1968 (The Beatles) & 22–23 October 1968 (George Martin), EMI and De Lane Lea Studios, London.
Producer: George Martin
Co-producers (orchestral score): John Burgess, Ron Richards
Engineers: Geoff Emerick, Eddie Kramer
Tracks: Yellow Submarine / Only A Northern Song / All Together Now / Hey Bulldog / It's All Too Much / All You Need Is Love / Pepperland / Sea Of Time / Sea Of Holes / Sea Of Monsters / March Of The Meanies / Pepperland Laid Waste / Yellow Submarine In Pepperland

---

"I love cartoons. I love the Disney stuff so you know the first thing when we heard people were going to do a cartoon I just thought, Yeah this could be the greatest Disney cartoon ever. I mean, with our music. But they were going more Pepper direction so we said, Well why don't you just take a lot of songs we've got already?" – **Paul McCartney**

The band originally envisaged releasing the four songs which made their debut in the soundtrack for the *Yellow Submarine* motion picture as an EP (along with the unreleased 'Across The Universe'). Instead, they opted to flesh things out with the title track, 'All You Need Is Love' and a specially recorded version of Martin's orchestral film score (which would later be binned in favour of the majority of the band's songs used in the film as the *Yellow Submarine Songtrack* in 1999). 'Across The Universe', for the time being, remained unreleased.

So, looking at the four new songs, we get two almost-anthems from Harrison ('Only A Northern Song' and 'It's All Too Much'), a balls-out rocker ('Hey Bulldog') and the kiddie sing-along that ends the film ('All Together Now'). On his collaboration with Lennon on 'Hey Bulldog', McCartney cited the crazy rap between the pair at the songs' end as being very much part of their 'say something once, why say it again?' mentality at the time – of trying to make every song unique.

The album was released in the UK on the same day as Led Zeppelin's debut album was released in the US.

GET BACK / DON'T LET ME DOWN

UK Release: Apple R 5777, 11 April 1969 (SP)
US Release: Apple 2490, 5 May 1969 (SP - first US single release in stereo)
Recording data: 21 – 30 January 1969, EMI Studios, London
Producer: George Martin
Engineer: Glyn Johns

"We were sitting in the studio and we made it up out of thin air... we started to write words there and then... when we finished it, we recorded it at Apple Studios and made it into a song to roller-coast by." – **Paul McCartney**

Following release of "The White Album", the Beatles planned to make a TV show featuring performances of tracks from that record. This quickly transmuted into creating a new collection of songs for a televised concert. They then decided to film their rehearsals for this new music, so that viewers could see the songs evolve.

Finally, they tweaked things some more so that the thrilling denouement to this project would be a return to live performance - without a net, and no overdubs: viz, the famous rooftop concert on the *Apple* building at 3 Savile Row, London. On my eleventh birthday. Oh yes.

Get Back was to have been the title for the resultant television show and album – based on McCartney's scheme to 'get back' to the band's roots. Lennon came up with the idea of the hirsute 1969 Beatles adopting the pose from the *Please Please Me* album, with the band looking down the stairwell of *EMI's* London offices in Manchester Square, for the cover of the new record. According to Mal Evans, they even re-made 'Love Me Do' for this venture.

However, by the end of January, the whole shebang was abandoned. It was of course resurrected a year later (renamed *Let It Be*), and the group photo eventually wound up on the front of the 1967-1970 'blue album' cover. But I'm jumping ahead.
This single snuck out as the first fruits from this scrapped venture and, if we discount the recordings made with Tony Sheridan (and we really should – they're not all that), is the one and only Beatles' record to be credited to the band with A.N. Other – organist Billy Preston.

In 1969, Harrison went to see Ray Charles in concert in London. Part of Charles' backing band that night was Preston, who The Beatles had first met in Hamburg while he was playing organ for Little Richard in nineteen-dickety-two. Harrison thought the chirpy Preston might help ease the tensions growing within the band, and brought him back to the studio. It did seem to help, and at one time Lennon pondered making him the official fifth Beatle. This notion was quickly pooh-poohed by McCartney, who realised the end was nigh.

With Preston's presence, it's odd that accusations of racism continue to be levelled at McCartney over this song. Early demo versions included references to immigrants in Britain, but McCartney has always claimed these were critical of attitudes in the country at the time. It's called satire, people.

Anyway, like the whole *Get Back* idea, the lyrics went through various permutations before McCartney hit upon the final tale of Jo Jo and the sexually confused Loretta Martin. A rocking little number for sure, with Lennon playing lead guitar. It entered the UK charts at number one – another first for the band.

While Lennon did ponder whether McCartney was singing "get back to where you once belonged" to Yoko, his own b-side was most certainly aimed at her. An angst-ridden plea for his bride-to-be to justify his devotion to her.

These two songs are arguably the best of the batch from the dynamic duo, yet producer Phil Spector amazingly ignored 'Don't Let Me Down' when he was brought in to make sense of the Get Back session tapes.

In the press release for the single, McCartney wrote "In 'Get Back' and 'Don't Let Me Down', you'll find The Beatles, as nature intended," – a sentiment he would hark back to over 30 years later with the release of *Let It Be... Naked* - which rightfully restored 'Don't Let Me Down' to album status.

This was the first Beatles single to be released in stereo in the US. In the UK, it was released a week after the first Plastic Ono Band single, Give Peace A Chance – which was credited to Lennon/McCartney, though in fact it was actually composed by Lennon with Ono.

During the making of *Let It Be*, 1969 © Daily Sketch / Rex

THE BALLAD OF JOHN AND YOKO / OLD BROWN SHOE

UK Release: Apple R 5786, 30 May 1969 (SP)
US Release: Apple 2531, 4 June 1969 (SP)
Recording data: 14, 16, 18 April 1969 EMI Studios, London
Producer: George Martin
Engineer: Geoff Emerick

"How can I be lonely when I'm with Yoko day and night? I'm lonely in the universal sense, but there are no outside desires. We are the best things we can give each other."
- John Lennon

The a-side was recorded and performed in one day, solely by Lennon and McCartney - with Lennon apparently referring to McCartney as 'Ringo', and McCartney calling Lennon 'George', during the session. McCartney later talked of his surprise that it still "ended up sounding like The Beatles" despite the absence of Starr and Harrison.

The song details the events surrounding Lennon's marriage to Ono on 20 March 1969, and was penned by Lennon on his honeymoon. Laughable now, but the chorus ("Christ, you know it ain't easy...") was quite controversial in 1969 and the record did get banned/bleeped by some radio stations.

It was to be the band's last 45 to top the charts, and their first to be released in stereo in the UK and Europe.

Harrison composed the b-side on piano, and played *Hammond* organ and bass (as well as lead guitar) on the recording. Like 'Hello, Goodbye', the words were based around various opposites (right/wrong, up/down) though a lot less overtly - as a matter of fact, I always found the lyrics a little indistinct and it seems Harrison plonked himself down in the corner of the studio to get a more conspiratorial sound.

ABBEY ROAD

UK Release: Apple (Parlophone) PCS 7088, 26 September 1969 (LP)
US Release: Apple (Capitol) SO 383, 1 October 1969 (LP)
Recording data: 22 February – 20 August 1969 EMI, Olympic and Trident Studios, London.
Producer: George Martin
Engineers: Geoff Emerick, Phil McDonald, Alan Parsons
Tracks: Come Together / Something / Maxwell's Silver Hammer / Oh! Darling / Octopus's Garden / I Want You (She's So Heavy) / Here Comes the Sun / Because / You Never Give Me Your Money / Sun King / Mean Mr. Mustard / Polythene Pam / She Came in Through the Bathroom Window / Golden Slumbers / Carry That Weight / The End / Her Majesty

---

"The last section of Abbey Road I still think as, for me, one of the finest pieces we put together." – **Ringo Starr**

"I liked the a-side but I never liked that sort of pop opera on the other side. I think it's just because it was just bits of songs thrown together." – **John Lennon**

The disastrous sessions for the abandoned *Get Back* album saw the band members working more and more in isolation. With tensions running high, at McCartney's instigation the group agreed to put their differences to one side and make an album together – like they used to in the early days. Well, well. George Martin insisted on playing a greater role, and together they came up with possibly the most cohesive album of their career. This may have been due in part to the fact that all four perceived this to be their swan song. It wasn't; as you will read (if you don't already know), Get Back was re-made/re-modelled to become the album *Let It Be...* which in turn was refashioned into *Let It Be... Naked* many, many years later.

But we're talking *Abbey Road* here. And it opens presciently enough with Lennon's 'Come Together', another excellent example of his word association football. Some say the four verses reference the four Fabs, but Lennon himself claimed the lyrics were gobbledygook, while recognising it as "one of my favourite Beatle tracks, or, one of my favourite Lennon tracks, let's say that. It's funky, it's bluesy, and I'm singing it pretty well. I like the sound of the record. You can dance to it. I'd buy it!" It is also a favourite of producer George Martin's.

True to going back to their roots, the song owes a debt to Chuck Berry's 'You Can't Catch Me'. Throughout (before each verse, and the organ and end guitar solo) Lennon sings "Shoot me", a plea for a heroin fix, apparently. As noted by Tony Barrow, at the time Lennon was well on his way to becoming a full-blown drug addict. He admitted to having had over a thousand LSD trips since 1964, and 12 months prior to the release of Abby Road, he and Yoko had been busted for possession of marijuana, the drug that had been such an inspiration on the band's lyrics over the past few years. But his heroin use was relatively new and explains his comparatively minimal input to this album. He later acknowledged, "We sniffed a little when we were in real pain. We got such a hard time from everyone, and I've had so much thrown at me and at Yoko, especially at Yoko. We took H because of what the Beatles and others were doing to us." So it was everyone's fault but his. We should be ashamed of ourselves. Poor long lost John.

Anyway, a cracking tune and a fine way to kick off their last great album. Lennon's lack of focus meant that Harrison again got to have two songs included on a single album, and what a lovely pair!

'Something' was written while the Beatles were recording "The White Album". Although Harrison would later claim he was thinking more about Ray Charles when he wrote it. In her wonderful 2007 autobiography, *Wonderful Tonight: George Harrison, Eric Clapton And Me*, Harrison's first wife Pattie recalls that, "He told me, in a matter-of-fact way, that he had written it for me. I thought it was beautiful – and it turned out to be the most successful song he ever wrote, with more than a hundred and fifty cover versions. His favourite was the one by James Brown. Frank Sinatra said he thought it was the best love song ever written." But Sinatra used to mistakenly introduce it as a Lennon/McCartney composition. Pratt. According to Harrison, Michael Jackson also made the same mistake. As engineer Emerick noted when Harrison first brought the song into the studio, "For the first time, John and Paul knew that George had risen to their level."

As well as 'Something', Pattie was the inspiration for Eric Clapton's 'Layla'. Can you imagine having just one song of that calibre penned for you, let alone two? Obviously Clapton also penned 'Wonderful Tonight' for Pattie, but I wouldn't place that particular soft-rock classic in the same league as the other two. Would you?

Harrison openly admitted that 'Something' took its first line from a track on James Taylor's eponymous debut album for *Apple*, *Something In The Way She Moves* (which Taylor had originally wanted to call 'I Feel Fine'!).

Next up, a bit of McCartney "granny music", which an overly serious Lennon refused to play on. 'Maxwell's Silver Hammer' is just a bit of sing-along fluff, true, but they (the other three) spent a long time getting it just right in the studio, including early use of a Moog synthesizer. Another of McCartney's story songs. Harmless fun. Lighten up, people. 'Oh! Darling' is better, and one of McCartney's that Lennon wanted to sing. But didn't. Featuring impressive three-part vocal harmonies, the song may have been influenced by Frank Zappa & The Mothers of Invention's recently released *Cruising With Ruben & The Jets*, which itself was a homage to 1950s doo wop and rock and roll. McCartney's vocal is intentionally raw, harking back to his live stabs at 'Long Tall Sally' and 'I'm Down'.

Starr's second (and final) solo composition for The Beatles was written when he temporarily walked out of the band and took his family for a boating holiday: "I wrote 'Octopus's Garden' in Sardinia. Peter Sellers had lent us his yacht and we went out for the day. I stayed out on deck with [the captain] and we talked about octopuses. He told me that they hang out in their caves and they go around the seabed finding shiny stones and tin cans and bottles to put in front of their cave like a garden. I thought this was fabulous, because at the time I just wanted to be under the sea too. A couple of tokes later, and we had 'Octopus's Garden'!"

Thematically linked to 'Yellow Submarine' and, like 'Maxwell's Silver Hammer', another lightweight ditty. But enjoyable nonetheless. Musically, Harrison helped Starr with the arrangement a tad in the studio, as well as adding bubble sound effects by blowing through a straw in a glass of milk.

'I Want You (She's So Heavy)' is Lennon's intentionally simple and direct tip of the hat to his all consuming love for Ono. The music may be repetitive and undemanding, but it builds and builds until it... just eerily cuts off. At eight minutes long, it may be a bit much for some; I recall, having belatedly caught up with the Fabs in the twilight of their career, my brother and I played this entire album to our parents to show them how the boys had progressed since the height of Beatlemania. But we turned this one off half way through. For their benefit. I personally love this song, and it could have gone on longer. The final overdub session for this track was the last time all four Beatles worked in the studio together.

Side two starts with Harrison's second contribution, 'Here Comes The Sun', a song written while visiting his friend Eric Clapton at his Italian-style villa, Hurtwood Edge, in the Surrey stockbroker belt. In his autobiography, Clapton describes it as one of

Harrison's most beautiful songs, and remembers its conception thusly: "It was a beautiful spring morning and we were sitting at the top of a big paddock at the bottom of the garden. We had our guitars and were just strumming away when he started singing, 'De da de de, it's been a long cold lonely winter,' and bit by bit fleshed it out, until the first verse was finished and it was time for lunch." Hum dee dum dee dum.

Another beauty from Harrison, indeed proving his old comment that if Lennon and McCartney could do it, so could he.

'Because' is another gem on the side of the album where there really are no clunkers. Having previously told Beethoven to roll over, here Lennon claims they reversed the chords to a bit of the old Ludwig Van's Piano Sonata No. 14 in C-sharp minor "Quasi una fantasia", Op. 27, No. 2 (better known simply as the 'Moonlight Sonata'), and added glorious triple tracked three part harmony vocals - which Harrison and McCartney in particular took extra care to get right as they knew they were working on something special; it was, purportedly, their favourite song on the whole album. And it leads straight into what this author and many others consider a work of genius – principally by McCartney and Martin, who stitched together the thrilling denouement that is the *Abbey Road* medley.

The famous second side medley exists of 'You Never Give Me Your Money' (McCartney's dig at recently appointed *Apple Corps* manager, Allen Klein), 'Sun King' (inspired by Fleetwood Mac's 'Albatross' and featuring cod-Spanish twaddle from Lennon), 'Mean Mr. Mustard' (written in India and dismissed by composer Lennon as "crap"), 'Polythene Pam' (Mr Mustard's sister, into kinky sex), 'She Came in Through The Bathroom Window' (based on a real life incident when a girl fan broke into McCartney's Cavendish Avenue home, recorded as one with the previous track), 'Golden Slumbers' (with lyrics liberated by McCartney from a ballad by the Elizabethan poet, Thomas Dekker), 'Carry That Weight' (recorded as one with the previous track, with Harrison on bass and Lennon away recovering in hospital following a road accident in Scotland) and 'The End' (starting with Starr's sole solo for the band on his chosen instruments and peaking with the other three sparring on lead guitars).

Regarding the guitar solos, engineer Emerick noted its spontaneity, with everybody saying yes, "except for George, who was a little apprehensive at first. But he saw how excited John and Paul were so he went along with it. Truthfully, I think they rather liked the idea of playing together, not really trying to outdo one another per se, but engaging in some real musical bonding. Yoko was about to go into the studio with John - this was commonplace by now - and he actually told her, 'No, not now. Let me just do this. It'll just take a minute.' That surprised me a bit. Maybe he felt like he was returning to his roots with the boys - who knows? They ran down their ideas a few times and before you knew it, they were ready to go. Their amps were lined up together and we recorded their parts on one track. You could really see the joy in their faces as they played; it was like they were teenagers again. One take was all we needed. The musical telepathy between them was mind-boggling."

Most of the constituent parts of the medley were incomplete songs, which McCartney swept up into one 16-minute sequence. It would have been a fitting end to their recording career, were it not for the fact that they still had *Let It Be* up their sleeves, as well as a small chunk excised from the medley...

'Her Majesty' was possibly the first... I mean second... 'hidden' track in rock, although it was actually listed on later releases. (The first hidden track was of course the 'dog cut' – or "Sgt. Pepper Inner Groove" as it became known) Originally a part of the medley (between 'Mean Mr. Mustard' and 'Polythene Pam'), McCartney had edited out 'Her

Majesty' and the tape operator appended it to the end of the reel, with a 14 second lead-out to separate it from the rest of the recording. On hearing the whole tape on playback, McCartney liked the effect so much that it stayed a part of the album. The final track on the final Beatles' album-proper is also the shortest, at just 23 seconds long.

At the time of *Abbey Road*, Lennon said of his songwriting partnership with McCartney "We haven't written together for two years. Not really, anyway... you know, occasional bits - a line or two. It doesn't make any odds: when the Beatles perform, that makes it Beatlemusic. We used to write mainly on tours. Today the Beatles just go into a studio, and IT happens!"

The album was released in the US on the day Concorde first broke the sound barrier.

SOMETHING / COME TOGETHER

UK Release: Apple R 5814, 31 October 1969 (SP)
US Release: Apple 2654, 1 October 1969 (SP)
Recording data: 25 February, 16 April, 2 May, 21–30 July & 15 August 1969, EMI Studios, London
Producer: George Martin
Engineer: Geoff Emerick

"Something was written on the piano while we were making The White Album. I had a break while Paul was doing some overdubbing so I went into an empty studio and began to write. It didn't go on The White Album because we'd already finished all the tracks."
- George Harrison

"Come Together was an expression that Leary had come up with for his attempt at being president or whatever he wanted to be, and he asked me to write a campaign song. I tried and tried, but I couldn't come up with one. But I came up with this." **– John Lennon**

Released as a double a-side in the UK, marking the only time that a 7 incher was taken from an already released Beatles album in this country. All Allen Klein's doing, apparently. It peaked at number 4, making it the band's first single since 'Love Me Do' that failed to get into the top two. But there have been many travesties since – like Joe Dolce Music Theatre's 'Shaddap You Face' keeping Ultravox's 'Vienna' from the top spot – and they'll be many more in the future thanks to X Factor.

Klein was the American businessman brought in by Lennon to try and stem the flow of cash leaking out of *Apple* in 1969. Lennon had convinced Starr and Harrison that Klein was the man for the job - but not McCartney, who had wanted his father-in-law Lee Eastman to sort out their financial mess. Despite his misgivings, McCartney was though happy to sign a new contract with *EMI*, negotiated by Klein which saw the band getting the highest royalties ever paid to an artist.

This single was Klein's first action to bring in urgently needed money to *Apple*. It was released a week after the Plastic One Band's 'Cold Turkey' single – whose failure to reach higher than number 13 in the charts prompted Lennon to return his MBE in protest. Well, that, and the war in Biafra.

NO ONE'S GONNA CHANGE OUR WORLD

UK Release: Regal Starline SRS 5013, 12 December 1969 (LP)
Recording data: 4 February 1968, Abbey Road Studios, London
Producer: George Martin
Engineers: Martin Benge, Ken Scott, Peter Bown
Tracks: Across the Universe (The Beatles) / What the World Needs Now Is Love (Cilla Black) / Cuddly Old Koala (Rolf Harris) / Wings (The Hollies) / Ning Nang Nong (Spike Milligan) / The Python (Spike Milligan) / Marley Purt Drive (Bee Gees) / I'm a Tiger (Lulu) / Bend It (Dave Dee, Dozy, Beaky, Mick & Tich) / In the Country (Cliff Richard) / When I See an Elephant Fly (Bruce Forsyth) / Land of My Fathers (Harry Secombe)

'Across The Universe' was written by Lennon late at night after an argument with Cynthia: "It drove me out of bed, I didn't want to write it. I was just slightly irritable and I couldn't go to sleep." Recorded during the sessions for 'Lady Madonna', Lennon hoped to release it as a single, but complained that "it wasn't a very good recording." He later added that "We'd always play experimental games with my great pieces, like 'Strawberry Fields Forever' – which I always felt was recorded badly. That song got away with it and worked. But usually we'd spend hours doing little detailed clean-ups of Paul's songs; but when it came to mine, especially if it was a great song like "Strawberry Fields" or 'Across The Universe', somehow this atmosphere of looseness and casualness and experimentation would creep in."

In the case of 'Across The Universe', instead of hiring professional singers for the background vocals, McCartney enlisted the help of two girl fans, sixteen-year-old Lizzie Bravo from Brazil and seventeen-year-old Gayleen Pease from London. Engineer Benge recalls, "They were so excited. They couldn't believe they'd actually been invited by Paul not just inside the building but into the studio itself, to sing with The Beatles." But Lennon grumbled that they sang off-key, and later declared the recording "a real piece of shit".

With no room on "The White Album" for the track, the band decided to donate it to charity - for an album compiled by former Goon/comic genius, Spike Milligan, for the benefit of the World Wildlife Fund. The album was named after a bowdlerised line from the song, and featured liner notes by none other than Prince Philip. But Lennon still protested that the World Wildlife Fund "didn't do much with it," and resurrected it later.

THE BEATLES' SEVENTH CHRISTMAS RECORD: HAPPY CHRISTMAS 1969

UK Release: Lyntone LYN 1970/1971, 19 December 1969 (SP)
Recording data: November–December 1969, various locations.
Producer: Maurice Cole

With the band now effectively disbanded, this final Christmas record is dominated by John and Yoko recorded in and around their Tittenhurst Park estate. All rather aimless and meandering. Starr and McCartney have a bit of a sing (as do John & Yoko), while Harrison makes the briefest of brief appearances.

Starr also gets to plug *The Magic Christian*, his recent film co-starring Peter Sellers for which McCartney wrote and produced the song 'Come And Get It' (performed by doomed *Apple* band, Badfinger). The film also features a cameo from Roman Polanski.

On 18 December the following year, *Apple* munificently decided to give each fan club member on both sides of the Atlantic a free vinyl LP containing all seven singles – with different titles: From Then To You in the UK (Lyntone LYN 2153/4) and The Beatles' Christmas Album in the US (SBC-100).

Ringo at the premiere of the film *The Magic Christian*, London, December 1969 © Harry Myers / Rex

HEY JUDE

US Release: Apple (Capitol) SO-385, 26 February 1970 (LP)
UK Release: Apple (Parlophone) PCS 7184, 11 May 1979 (LP)
Recording data: 1964–1969, EMI and Trident Studios, London and Pathé Marconi Studio, Paris
Producer: George Martin
Engineer: Norman Smith, Geoff Emerick, Ken Scott, Barry Sheffield, Glyn Johns
Tracks: Can't Buy Me Love / I Should Have Known Better / Paperback Writer / Rain / Lady Madonna / Revolution / Hey Jude / Old Brown Shoe / Don't Let Me Down / The Ballad Of John And Yoko

---

Originally to be titled *The Beatles Again*, *Hey Jude* is a compilation of non-album singles and b-sides conceived by Klein to boost Apple's coffers. It focuses on more recent material and as such is a fairly arbitrary collection.

Although the album was not released in the UK until 1979, it was made available as an 'export' from Britain (*Apple* (*Parlophone*), CPCS-106) in February 1970; in the interim, it was a popular 'import' in this country.

The cover pictures were taken at the last-ever Beatles photo session in the grounds of Lennon's Tittenhurst Park estate.

LET IT BE / YOU KNOW MY NAME (LOOK UP THE NUMBER)

UK Release: Apple R 5833, 6 March 1970 (SP)
US Release: Apple 2764, 11 March 1970 (SP)
Recording data: 17 May, 7 and 8 June 1967, 31 January and 30 April 1969 & 4 January 1970, Apple and EMI Studios, London
Producer: George Martin
Engineer: Glyn Johns, Geoff Emerick

"One night during this tense time I had a dream I saw my mum, who'd been dead 10 years or so. It was so wonderful for me and she was very reassuring. In the dream she said, 'It'll be all right.' So that got me writing the song..." – **Paul McCartney**

The Beatles' final single before McCartney formally announced his departure from the band. How apt.

A piano-led ballad that had a glorious swelling organ smack dab in the middle (courtesy of Preston) and backing vocals performed by Lennon and Harrison... and Linda McCartney. Odd then that its composer would say a month after its relelase that he "would never have female voices on a Beatles record," when presented with Phil Spector's remix of his song 'The Long And Winding Road'.

While undoubtedly a fan favourtie, Lennon was very dismissive of 'Let It Be' - comparing it unfavourably to Simon & Garfunkel's classic, 'Bridge Over Troubled Water' (released a couple of months earlier).

A very anthemic song, McCartney would close the Live Aid charity concert at Wembley with a solo rendition of 'Let It Be' in 1986, before an estimated global TV audience of one billion people. It would also become the grand finale of the stripped down/rebooted *Let It Be... Naked* album some 33 years hence.

The single reached number two in the UK charts, but McCartney had greater success with it seventeen years later when he was part of the Ferry Aid supergroup that recorded it to raise funds for the families of the 193 passengers and crew who lost their lives when the Herald of Free Enterprise ferry capsized in the Belgian port of Zeebrugge.

Lennon originally wanted to release the b-side as the a-side of a single by the Plastic One Band (coupled with "White Album" outtake, 'What's The New Mary Jane') - which went as far as being allocated *Apple* catalogue number 1002. But it was not to be. 'You Know My Name (Look Up The Number)' remains the oddest thing ever to be released by the Beatles – and I most certainly include 'Revolution 9'.

Recorded over a two-year period, Lennon was inspired to produce this 'comedy record' after seeing the tagline on the front of a phone book. It features roadie Mal Evans on 'spade in gravel' and Rolling Stone Brian Jones on alto saxophone; Jones would be dead by the time of the record's release and Evans would be shot dead by the LAPD six years later.

Both sides of this record are so far removed from the first Beatles' singles that a visiting alien wouldn't have recognised it as the same band.

The US release of' Let It Be' came the day before the first wedding anniversary of the McCartneys.

LET IT BE

UK Release: Apple (Parlophone) PCS 7096, 8 May 1970 (LP)
US Release: Apple (Capitol) AR-34001, 18 May 1970 (LP)
Recording data: February 1968, January–February 1969, January and March–April 1970, EMI and Apple studios and Twickenham Film Studios, London
Producer: Phil Spector
Engineers: Glyn Johns, Martin Benge, Ken Scott, Peter Bown, Phil McDonald, Jeff Jarratt
Tracks: Two Of Us / Dig A Pony / Across The Universe / I Me Mine / Dig It / Let It Be / Maggie Mae / I've Got A Feeling / One After 909 / The Long And Winding Road / For You Blue /Get Back

---

"In a nutshell, it was time for another Beatle movie or something, and Paul wanted us to go on the road or do something. As usual, George and I were going, Oh, we don't want to do it, fuck, and all that. He set it up and there was all discussions about where to go and all that. I would just tag along and I had Yoko by then, I didn't even give a shit about anything. I was stoned all the time, too, on H etc. And I just didn't give a shit. And nobody did, you know. Anyway, it's like in the movie where I go to do 'Across The Universe', Paul yawns and plays boogie, and I merely say, Oh, anybody want to do a fast one?" – **John Lennon**

Most of the recording for this album (as mentioned before, originally to be titled *Get Back*) took place at their new *Apple* Studios in Savile Row throughout January of 1969. Many hours and mulitple takes of original material and cover versions were committed to tape, but with Lennon perpetually out of it, Harrison increasingly disinterested in working on anyone else's songs but his own and Starr pursuing outside film work, the album was temporarily abandoned at the end of the month.

The fraught sessions saw a second band member temporarily walk out, as Harrison felt insulted by Lennon's obsession with Ono. On 10 January 1969, Harrison told Lennon he was leaving the band immediately. A week later, he agreed to return on condition that the band didn't do a live concert abroad and that they stop filming at the "dreary Twickenham studios." As mentioned earlier, he brought Billy Preston with him.

Regarding the flamboyant Preston, it seems he could on occasion be a little over-exuberant. Like the time Keith Richards had to pull a blade on him, when he was the Rolling Stones' touring keyboardist in the mid-70s, for playing too loudly and trying to steal the show. This is detailed in Richards' riotous autobiography, Life. As this is not the first time I've mentioned that particular book, I think it's clear that I think you should read it - if you haven't already. Straight after you finish this one, naturally.

Anyway, in March 1970, after failed attempts by engineer Glyn Johns to piece together a workable album, the tapes were handed over to American producer Phil Spector to create a new version. The result was re-titled *Let It Be*, and it served as the 'soundtrack' for the 1970 motion picture of the same name, released the same day.

With three George Martin-produced songs from the sessions having already been issued on singles, Spector chose to remix two of these ('Let It Be' and 'Get Back', utilising a far tastier Harrison guitar solo on the former) and dumped Lennon's 'Don't Let Me Down'.

The album opens with 'Two Of Us', a song ostensibly about McCartney and his then wife to be, though it also reflects on his relationship with Lennon. While a version of Harrison's 'I Me Mine' appears in the film, the one on the album was recorded at *EMI's* studios in Abbey Road in January 1970 while Lennon was on holiday. This was effectively the last song to be recorded by The Beatles... until 1994.

McCartney was the only band member not happy with *Let It Be* - especially the overdubbed orchestra and female vocals on his beautiful ballad, 'The Long And Winding Road'.

With the original recordings being overseen by Martin, 'the fifth Beatle' wanted to see the album credits amended to "Produced by George Martin and overproduced by Phil Spector"!

Lennon leapt to Spector's defence, saying that he had been given "shit, and made something of it."

Both Lennon and Harrison's initial post-Beatle albums would be produced by Spector, and Starr admitted he liked what the producer had done

Let It Be of course sold well, and is regarded as their final album despite being largely recorded before *Abbey Road* and released after the band had formally disbanded.

Very few people, if any, would regard it as their finest 35 minutes, though it does end amusingly with Lennon's rooftop sign-off of, "I'd like to say 'thank you' on behalf of the group and ourselves, and I hope we passed the audition."

FROM THEN TO YOU (THE BEATLES' CHRISTMAS ALBUM)

UK Release: Apple (Lyntone) LYN 2153/4, 18 December 1970 (LP)
US Release: Apple (Lyntone) SBC-100, 18 December 1970 (LP)
Recording data: 1963–1969, various locations
Producers: Tony Barrow, George Martin, Kenny Everett, Maurice Cole
Tracks: The Beatles' Christmas Record / Another Beatles Christmas Record / The Beatles' Third Christmas Record / The Beatles' Fourth Christmas Record – Pantomime: Everywhere It's Christmas / Christmas Time is Here Again! / The Beatles' 1968 Christmas Record / The Beatles' Seventh Christmas Record: Happy Christmas 1969

Apple munificently decided to give each fan club member on both sides of the Atlantic a free vinyl LP containing all seven Christmas fan club singles – with different titles: *From Then To You* in the UK; *The Beatles' Christmas Album* in the US.

1962–1966

UK Release: Apple (EMI) SKBO 3403, 2 April 1973 (LP)
US Release: Apple (Capitol) PCSP 717, 19 April 1973 (LP)
Recording data: 1962–1966, EMI Studios, London and Pathé Marconi Studios, Paris
Producer: George Martin
Engineers: Norman Smith, Geoff Emerick
Tracks: Love Me Do / Please Please Me / From Me To You / She Loves You / I Want To Hold Your Hand / All My Loving / Can't Buy Me Love / A Hard Day's Night / And I Love Her / Eight Days A Week / I Feel Fine /Ticket To Ride / Yesterday / Help! / You've Got To Hide Your Love Away / We Can Work It Out / Day Tripper / Drive My Car / Norwegian Wood (This Bird Has Flown) / Nowhere Man / Michelle / In My Life / Girl / Paperback Writer / Eleanor Rigby / Yellow Submarine

---

"The Red Album", released at the same time as "The Blue Album" (1962-1967), was compiled by Allen Klein and comprised songs entirely composed by Lennon and McCartney, and principally the band's hit singles during the period. It's very interesting that the two albums very neatly split between the 'silly love song' and the more serious studio band eras.

1967–1970

UK Release: Apple (EMI) SKBO 3404, 2 April 1973 (LP)
US Release: Apple (Capitol) PCSP 718, 19 April 1973 (LP)
Recording data: 1966–1970, EMI, Olympic, Apple and Trident Studios, London
Producer: George Martin, Phil Spector
Engineers: Geoff Emerick, Eddie Kramer, Ken Scott, Barry Sheffield, Ken Townsend, Glyn Johns, Phil McDonald, Alan Parsons
Tracks: Strawberry Fields Forever / Penny Lane / Sgt. Pepper's Lonely Hearts Club Band / With A Little Help From My Friends / Lucy In The Sky With Diamonds / A Day In The Life / All You Need Is Love / I Am The Walrus / Hello, Goodbye / The Fool On The Hill / Magical Mystery Tour / Lady Madonna / Hey Jude / Revolution / Back In The U.S.S.R. / While My Guitar Gently Weeps / Ob-La-Di, Ob-La-Da / Get Back / Don't Let Me Down / The Ballad Of John And Yoko / Old Brown Shoe / Here Comes The Sun / Come Together / Something / Octopus's Garden / Let It Be / Across The Universe / The Long And Winding Road

---

"I didn't want lousy versions going out, I wanted them to be as was. I made sure George Martin was there and I made sure they put that picture... of the same pose as the very first album. So I don't mind that one. Checked the remix after he'd done it, it was as good as you could get out of whatever mono recording we did then." **– John Lennon**

"The Blue Album", released at the same time as "The Red Album" (1962-1966), was compiled by Allen Klein and comprised only songs penned by the band, and principally the band's hit singles during the period.

YESTERDAY / I SHOULD HAVE KNOWN BETTER

UK Release: Parlophone R 6013, 8 March 1976 (SP)
Recording data: 25, 26 February 1964 and 14, 17 June 1965, EMI Studios, London
Producer: George Martin
Engineer: Norman Smith

In 1976, as its nine year contract with The Beatles was about to expire, *EMI* reissued all 22 of the band's UK singles, plus this new one. Each was issued in a green cardboard sleeve similar to the original *Parlophone* paper ones, with a different colour picture of the group on the reverse. The complete set of 45s was issued as *The Singles Collection 1962-1970.*

ROCK 'N' ROLL MUSIC

UK Release: Parlophone PCSP 719, 11 June 1976 (LP)
US Release: Capitol SKBO 11537, 7 June 1976 (LP)
Recording data: 1962–1970, EMI and Apple studios, London
Producer: George Martin, Phil Spector
Engineers: Norman Smith, Geoff Emerick
Tracks: Twist And Shout / I Saw Her Standing There / You Can't Do That / I Wanna Be Your Man / I Call Your Name / Boys / Long Tall Sally / Rock And Roll Music / Slow Down / Medley: Kansas City-Hey, Hey, Hey, Hey! / Money (That's What I Want) / Bad Boy / Matchbox / Roll Over Beethoven / Dizzy Miss Lizzy / Any Time At All / Drive My Car / Everybody's Trying To Be My Baby / The Night Before / I'm Down / Revolution / Back In The U.S.S.R. / Helter Skelter / Taxman / Got To Get You Into My Life / Hey Bulldog / Birthday / Get Back

---

The first Beatles album to include the b-side of the 'Help!' single. I wasn't down: I bought it!

The band hated the album's artwork, which prompted Ringo to complain, "It made us look cheap and we never were cheap. All that Coca-Cola and cars with big fins was the Fifties!" Lennon offered to redesign it, suggesting that an old photo by Jürgen Vollmer (who had befriended the band in Hamburg, along with Astrid Kirchherr and Klaus Voormann in the early 60s) be used. Lennon himself had done just that for the cover of his own Rock 'N' Roll solo album the previous year.

In October 1980, this double-album was rent in twain with volumes one and two being issued as budget albums on both sides of the Atlantic.

BACK IN THE U.S.S.R. / TWIST AND SHOUT

UK Release: Parlophone R 6016, 25 June 1976 (SP)
Recording data: 11 February 1963 and 22, 23 August 1968, EMI Studios, London
Producer: George Martin
Engineer: Norman Smith, Ken Scott

The 24th official single in the UK was released to help promote the *Rock 'N' Roll Music* double album. This was the first time a track had been taken from "The White Album" and released as a single. It appeared in the same style green picture sleeve as the "Singles Collection" series.

LIVE! AT THE STAR-CLUB IN HAMBURG, GERMANY; 1962

German/UK Release: Bellaphon BLS5560/Lingasong LNL, 18 April 1977 (LP)
US Release: Atlantic LS-2-7001, 13 June 1977 (LP)
Recording data: Late December 1962, Star-Club, Hamburg, Germany
Producer: Larry Grossberg
Engineers: Adrian Barber
Tracks: Introduction-I Saw Her Standing There / Roll Over Beethoven / Hippy Hippy Shake / Sweet Little Sixteen / Lend Me Your Comb / Your Feet's Too Big / Twist And Shout / Mr Moonlight / A Taste Of Honey / Bésame Mucho / Reminiscing / Medley: Kansas City-Hey, Hey, Hey, Hey! / Nothin' Shakin' (But The Leaves On The Trees) / To Know Her Is To Love Her / Little Queenie / Falling In Love Again (Can't Help It) / Ask Me Why / Be-Bop-A-Lula / Hallelujah I Love Her So / Red Sails In The Sunset / Everybody's Trying To Be My Baby / Matchbox / I'm Talking About You / Shimmy Like Kate / Long Tall Sally / I Remember You
Additional tracks on US LP version (which replaced I Saw Her Standing There / Twist and Shout / Reminiscing / Ask Me Why): I'm Gonna Sit Right Down and Cry (Over You) / Where Have You Been All My Life? / Till There Was You / Sheila

---

"One drunken person recording another bunch of drunks does not constitute business deals."
- George Harrison

In his memoir, *The Man Who Gave The Beatles Away*, former manager Williams tells how recordings of the band performing at Hamburg's Star-Club were recovered in a building due to be demolished in 1972. Williams states that the tapes (made by the Liverpool musician Ted "Kingsize" Taylor on a reel-to-reel recorder) captured the band "during three or four sessions over Christmas and New Year" of 1961. Initially, he tried to sell the tapes to Harrison and Starr "for a few thousand", so that an official Beatles album could be released. The pair rejected his idea, so he and Taylor eventually struck a deal with the head of *Buk Records*, Paul Murphy, who created the *Lingasong* label specifically for the project.

On release, the year of the recordings was correctly identified but still the notion persisted that Starr just happened to be sitting in with the band (see The Beatles Appreciation Society Magazine Book from July 1977). In actual fact, Christmas 1962 was four months after Starr had replaced Best, and the *Please Please Me* album was then in the can. The band was grudgingly fulfilling its contractual obligation to perform in Hamburg while 'Love Me Do' was doing the business for them back home.
What is therefore surprising is that they seemingly chose to play so few originals – and the two that do appear on the German/UK release ('I Saw Her Standing There' and 'Ask Me Why') were removed from the US release (although this may have been for legal reasons).

The Beatles objected to this album, but they were unable to prevent its release. Indeed, like the 'Sheridan' recordings, there have been numerous variations reissued by different labels since 1977, and it wasn't until 1998 that the band finally asserted themselves and were awarded full rights to the performances.

Whatever some might say, 'the Hamburg tapes' (as Williams refers to them) are an important snapshot of the band live before they hit big. The quality is undeniably lo-fi, but you can still just about decipher the between song banter.

THE BEATLES AT THE HOLLYWOOD BOWL

UK Release: Parlophone EMTV 4, 6 May 1977 (LP)
US Release: Capitol SMAS 11638, 4 May 1977 (LP)
Recording data: 23 August 1964 and 30 August 1965, Hollywood Bowl, Hollywood, California
Producer: George Martin
Engineers: Hugh Davies, Pete Abbott, Geoff Emerick
Tracks: Twist And Shout / She's A Woman / Dizzy Miss Lizzy / Ticket To Ride / Can't Buy Me Love / Things We Said Today / Roll Over Beethoven / Boys / A Hard Day's Night / Help! / All My Loving / She Loves You / Long Tall Sally

---

"The Hollywood Bowl was marvellous. It was the one we all enjoyed most, even though it wasn't the largest crowd - because it seemed so important. We got on, and it was a big stage, and it was great. We could be heard in a place like the Hollywood Bowl, even though the crowds were wild...good acoustics." – **John Lennon**

"There have been an awful lot of bootleg recordings made of Beatles concerts around the world and they've been in wide circulation. But when I listened to the Hollywood Bowl tapes, I was amazed at the rawness and vitality of The Beatles' singing. I enlisted the technical expertise of Geoff Emerick and we transferred the recordings from three-track to 24-track tapes. The two tapes combined 22 songs and we whittled these down to 13. Some tracks had to be discarded because the music was obliterated by the screams." – **George Martin**

For those of you who've not heard this album (at the time of writing, it has yet to be officially released on CD - and is not even listed at the official Beatles.com website), the tracks from the band's live shows on *Anthology* don't really give you the full impact of those screaming fans at the height of Beatlemania. This does. And as the screams fade in, it's a little like the jet noise at the beginning of 'Back In The U.S.S.R.' Only with Ed Sullivan shouting, "And now, here they are: The Beatles!"

And no wonder the band's live sets were so short... 'Twist And Shout' here clocks in at just one minute and twenty seconds!

LOVE SONGS

UK Release: Parlophone PCSP 721, 19 November 1977 (LP)
US Release: Capitol SKBL-11711, 21 October 1977 (LP)
Recording data: 1962–1970 at EMI and Apple Studios, London
Producer: George Martin, Phil Spector
Engineers: Norman Smith, Geoff Emerick et al
Tracks: Yesterday / I'll Follow The Sun / I Need You / Girl / In My Life / Words Of Love / Here, There And Everywhere / Something / And I Love Her / If I Fell / I'll Be Back / Tell Me What You See / Yes It Is / Michelle / It's Only Love / You're Going To Lose That Girl / Every Little Thing / For No One / She's Leaving Home / The Long And Winding Road / This Boy / Norwegian Wood (This Bird Has Flown) / You've Got To Hide Your Love Away / I Will / P.S. I Love You

---

Released a year after McCartney had suspected "that people would have had enough of silly love songs." Lovingly compiled by short-sighted executives with long pockets, the collection was quite nicely packaged.

What more can I say?

SGT. PEPPERS LONELY HEARTS CLUB BAND - WITH A LITTLE HELP FROM MY FRIENDS / A DAY IN THE LIFE

UK Release: Parlophone R 6022, 30 September 1978 (SP)
Recording data: 19, 20 January; 1, 2, 3, 10, 22 February; 3, 6, 29, 30 March 1967, EMI Studios, London
Producer: George Martin
Engineer: Geoff Emerick

The Beatles' 25th UK single, and the first to feature tracks from the "Sgt. Pepper" album. This was released to coincide with the British premiere of the Robert Stigwood film, *Sgt. Pepper's Lonely Hearts Club Band*, starring The Bee Gees and Peter Frampton. The film's soundtrack featured music from both the "Sgt Pepper" and *Abbey Road* albums, with George Martin acting as musical director, conductor, arranger and producer.

RARITIES (UK Version)

UK Release: Apple PSLP 261, 2 December 1978 (LP)
Recording data: 1962–1970 at EMI Studios, London, Pathé Marconi Studio, Paris; EMI Studios, Bombay.
Producer: George Martin
Engineers: Norman Smith, Geoff Emerick, Martin Benge, Ken Scott, Peter Bown, Glyn Johns
Tracks: Across The Universe / Yes It Is / This Boy / The Inner Light / I'll Get You / Thank You Girl / Komm, Gib Mir Deine Hand / You Know My Name (Look Up The Number) / Sie Liebt Dich / Rain / She's A Woman / Matchbox / I Call Your Name / Bad Boy / Slow Down / I'm Down / Long Tall Sally

---

Initially issued as part of "The Beatles Collection" box set, this collection of b-sides, the full contents of the UK-only 'Long Tall Sally' EP, the two German language tracks from 1964, the song initially recorded for a US only album ('Bad Boy') and the version of 'Across The Universe' on the *No One's Gonna Change Our World* charity compilation album, was later released individually and then made redundant by the later *Past Masters* collections.

RARITIES (US Version)

UK Release: Capitol SPRO-8969, 24 March 1980 (LP)
Recording data: 1962-1969, EMI Studios, London; Pathé Marconi Studios, Paris; EMI Studios, Bombay.
Producer: George Martin
Engineers: Norman Smith, Geoff Emerick, Martin Benge, Ken Scott, Peter Bown, Glyn Johns
Tracks: Love Me Do / Misery / There's A Place / Sie Liebt Dich / And I Love Her / Help! / I'm Only Sleeping / I Am The Walrus / Penny Lane / Helter Skelter / Don't Pass Me By / The Inner Light / Across The Universe / You Know My Name (Look Up The Number) / Sgt. Pepper Inner Groove

---

Inspired by the UK collection of non-album b-sides, EPs and other curios, this version of *Rarities* focuses on tracks not released on the US *Capitol* or *Apple* LPs, alternative versions and other songs not readily available in the country. It merits its own page simply because it replicates just three songs from the earlier version, and includes three songs that have never appeared on CD (the alternate stereo versions of 'And I Love Her', 'I Am the Walrus' and 'Penny Lane'). The final track also differs slightly from the CD version of "Sgt.Pepper" in that it excludes the 15 kilohertz tone. I only know this because my dog told me. Arf.

THE BEATLES' BALLADS

UK Release: Parlophone PCS 7214, 14 October 1980 (LP)
Recording data: 1962–1970 at EMI, Trident and Apple Studios, London
Producer: George Martin, Phil Spector
Engineers: Norman Smith, Geoff Emerick et al
Tracks: Yesterday / Norwegian Wood (This Bird Has Flown) / Do You Want To Know A Secret / For No One / Michelle / Nowhere Man / You've Got To Hide Your Love Away / Across The Universe / All My Loving / Hey Jude / Something / The Fool On The Hill / Till There Was You / Long And Winding Road / Here Comes The Sun / Blackbird / And I Love Her / She's Leaving Home / Here, There And Everywhere / Let It Be

---

Another compilation, similar to the previous *Love Songs* album. 'Across The Universe' is the "Wildlife" version from *No One's Gonna Change Our World*. The cover painting was created in 1968 for possible use on the "Doll's House/White Album".

REEL MUSIC

UK Release: Parlophone PCS 7218, 22 March 1982 (LP)
US Release: Capitol SV 12199, 22 March 1982 (LP)
Recording data: 1962–1970 at EMI, Trident and Apple Studios, London
Producer: George Martin, Phil Spector
Engineers: Norman Smith, Geoff Emerick et al.
Tracks: A Hard Day's Night / I Should Have Known Better / Can't Buy Me Love / And I Love Her / Help! / You've Got To Hide Your Love Away / Ticket To Ride / Magical Mystery Tour / I Am The Walrus / Yellow Submarine / All You Need Is Love / Let It Be / Get Back / The Long And Winding Road

---

Another compilation album featuring 'And I Love Her' and 'You've Got To Hide Your Love Away', as well as a selection of other songs featured in Beatles movies.

Reel Music was swiftly followed by a single in a picture sleeve with the same artwork. The a-side was 'The Beatles Movie Medley', an artificial concoction that stitched excerpts from 'Magical Mystery Tour', 'All You Need Is Love', 'You've Got to Hide Your Love Away', 'I Should Have Known Better', 'A Hard Day's Night', 'Ticket to Ride' and 'Get Back' together.

The b-side was 'I'm Happy Just To Dance With You' (which appeared in the *A Hard Day's Night* film but not *Reel Music*).

20 GREATEST HITS

UK Release: Parlophone PCTC 260, 18 October 1982 (LP)
US Release: Capitol SV 12245, 11 October 1982 (LP)
Recording data: 1962–1970 at EMI, Trident and Apple Studios, London and Pathé Marconi Studio, Paris
Producer: George Martin, Phil Spector
Engineers: Norman Smith, Geoff Emerick et al.
Tracks: Love Me Do / From Me To You / She Loves You / I Want To Hold Your Hand / Can't Buy Me Love / A Hard Day's Night / I Feel Fine / Ticket To Ride / Help! / Day Tripper / We Can Work It Out / Paperback Writer / Yellow Submarine / Eleanor Rigby / All You Need Is Love / Hello, Goodbye / Lady Madonna / Hey Jude / Get Back / The Ballad Of John And Yoko

---

The US version replaces 'From Me To You', 'Day Tripper', 'Yellow Submarine', 'Eleanor Rigby' and 'The Ballad Of John And Yoko' with 'Eight Days A Week', 'Yesterday', 'Penny Lane', 'Come Together', 'Let It Be' and 'The Long And Winding Road'; 'Hey Jude' also had to be edited down to five minutes. There is also a European version, but life is short...

A chronological collection of Lennon-McCartney songs that reached number one in the UK and US.

ONLY THE BEATLES...

UK Release: Parlophone SMMC 151, 1 June 1986 (MC)
Recording data: 4 September 1962 – 15 July 1968, EMI Studios, London
Producer: George Martin
Engineers: Norman Smith, Geoff Emerick
Tracks: Love Me Do / Twist And Shout / She Loves You / This Boy / Eight Days A Week / All My Loving / Ticket To Ride / Yes It Is / Ob-La-Di Ob-La-Da / Lucy In The Sky With Diamonds / And I Love Her / Strawberry Fields Forever

---

I am including this collectable curio partly because I own a copy, and also because it includes previously unreleased stereo versions of 'This Boy' and 'Yes It Is' (later to be included on *Past Masters, Volume One*). It is also the first and only time that a special pressing of Beatles songs was ever issued for the promotion of a commercial product.

Parlophone, in cahoots with *Heineken UK*, made this unique compilation available by sending in four ring pulls from special beer cans and a crossed postal order or cheque for £2.99 (£2.49 + 50p for postage and packing) made payable to 'Heineken Beatles Offer'. You could apply as many times as you liked, until the offer ended on 30 June.

Unfortunately, it seems *Heineken* did not have written permission to do this and *Apple* took legal action to have the product swiftly withdrawn. But I got one. Did I already mention that?

PAST MASTERS, VOLUME ONE

UK Release: Apple (Parlophone) CDP 7 90043 2, 7 March 1988 (CD)
Recording data: 4 September 1962 – 14 June 1965, EMI Studios, London & Pathé Marconi Studios, Paris
Producer: George Martin
Engineers: Norman Smith
Tracks: Love Me Do / From Me To You / Thank You Girl / She Loves You / I'll Get You / I Want To Hold Your Hand / This Boy / Komm, Gib Mir Deine Hand / Sie Liebt Dich / Long Tall Sally / I Call Your Name / Slow Down / Matchbox / I Feel Fine / She's A Woman / Bad Boy / Yes It Is / I'm Down

---

Expanding on the *Rarities* album idea by adding non-album a-sides, this album covered the period 1962 to 1965. This, and its sister (Volume Two), were worthwhile compilations at last – put together when the band's entire back catalogue was issued on CD for the first time.

A double LP vinyl set was released later that year.

PAST MASTERS, VOLUME TWO

UK Release: Apple (Parlophone) CDP 7 90044 2, 7 March 1988 (CD)
Recording data: 16 October 1965 – 30 April 1969
Producer: George Martin
Engineers: Geoff Emerick.
Tracks: Day Tripper / We Can Work It Out / Paperback Writer / Rain / Lady Madonna / The Inner Light / Hey Jude / Revolution / Get Back / Don't Let Me Down / The Ballad Of John And Yoko / Old Brown Shoe / Across The Universe / Let It Be / You Know My Name (Look Up The Number)

Expanding on the *Rarities* album idea by adding non-album a-sides of the band's singles, this album covered the period 1965 to 1970.

On 9 September 2009, *Apple/EMI* released a remastered version of the two volumes together as a stereo double-CD set, with a monophonic version in the *Mono Masters* box set issued shortly thereafter.

LIVE AT THE BBC

UK Release: Apple (Parlophone) 31796, 30 November 1994 (LP)
US Release: Apple (Capitol) 31796, 6 December 1994 (LP)
Recording data: 22 January 1963 – 26 May 1965, United Kingdom – London, mainly
Producer: Bryant Marriott, Bernie Andrews, Terry Henebery, Ian Grant, Ron Belchier, Keith Bateson
Executive Producer: George Martin

Tracks: "Beatle Greetings" / From Us To You / "Riding On A Bus" / I Got A Woman / Too Much Monkey Business / Keep Your Hands Off My Baby / I'll Be On My Way / Young Blood / A Shot Of Rhythm And Blues / Sure To Fall (In Love with You) / Some Other Guy / Thank You Girl / "Sha La La La La!" / Baby It's You / That's All Right, Mama / Carol / Soldier Of Love (Lay Down Your Arms) / "A Little Rhyme" / Clarabella / I'm Gonna Sit Right Down And Cry (Over You) / Crying, Waiting, Hoping / "Dear Wack!" / You've Really Got A Hold On Me / To Know Her Is To Love Her / A Taste Of Honey / Long Tall Sally / I Saw Her Standing There / The Honeymoon Song / Johnny B. Goode / Memphis, Tennessee / Lucille / Can't Buy Me Love / "From Fluff to You" / Till There Was You / "Crinsk Dee Night" / A Hard Day's Night / "Have a Banana!" / I Wanna Be Your Man / "Just a Rumour" / Roll Over Beethoven / All My Loving / Things We Said Today / She's A Woman / Sweet Little Sixteen / "1822!" / Lonesome Tears In My Eyes / Nothin' Shakin' / The Hippy Hippy Shake / Glad All Over / I Just Don't Understand / So How Come (No One Loves Me) / I Feel Fine / I'm A Loser / Everybody's Trying To Be My Baby / Rock And Roll Music / Ticket To Ride / Dizzy Miss Lizzy / Medley: Kansas City-Hey, Hey, Hey, Hey! / "Set Fire to That Lot!" / Matchbox / I Forgot To Remember to Forget / "Love These Goon Shows!" / I Got To Find My Baby / Ooh! My Soul / "Ooh! My Arms" / Don't Ever Change / Slow Down / Honey Don't / Love Me Do

---

"We wanted to be on Brian Matthews' Saturday Club. This was a huge radio show, and the thing I loved about listening to it was that I could wake up after a week of school and have a lie-in. The most delicious lie-ins of your life are those teenage lie-ins: wake up feeling great, turn the radio on and Saturday Club is still on for an hour. So we really wanted to be on that." – **Paul McCartney**

"We did a lot of tracks we'd been doing in the Cavern or Hamburg. There's some good stuff and they were well recorded." – **John Lennon**

Between 1962 and 1965, the band had 275 performances of 88 different songs broadcast by the *BBC*. During the intervening years, the 'Beeb' regularly aired excerpts from these sessions and I have cassettes of a number of these (incidentally, it was home-tapers like me – but not actually me – who helped plug some of the gaps in the *BBC's* archive). It was great to finally have an official compilation of the cream of the songs they performed, all spruced-up on CD. It's worth emphasising that, as should be clear from the opening statement above, many songs were performed on a number of different occasions. This is borne out by the second volume released nineteen years later, which included a baker's dozen of repeats. So both volumes together do not constitute anything like a comprehensive collection of their sessions. In fact, they first performed for the *BBC* before they had a recording contract and when Best was still in the band, but none of the recordings from 1962 have thus far been deemed suitable for release. Martin, who selected the songs for this first volume, was more interested in the quality of the recording and the band's performance than the historical significance of a particular piece.

While some of these songs were indeed recorded for established programmes like *Saturday Club* and *Easy Beat*, the Corporation dreamt up new shows befitting the band's increasing popularity to accommodate even more appearances. Thus these recordings are also taken from shows named *Pop Go The Beatles*, *From Us to You* and *The Beatles Invite You To Take A Ticket To Ride*.

Stand out tracks are largely the 30 ones not previously released by the band, especially the lesser-known songs like 'Soldier Of Love (Lay Down Your Arms)', 'Clarabella' and 'Lonesome Tears In My Eyes' (a song whose original intro by Johnny

Burnette & His Rock 'N Roll Trio influenced the guitar outro to 'The Ballad Of John & Yoko').

For those of us who had seen the grainy *Granada* Television clip of the band performing 'Some Other Guy' at The Cavern in 1962 (with the newly appointed Starr on drums), it was incredible to finally have a full recording of the song. And one similarly recorded in front of a live audience. The ousted Pete Best tried to capitalise on this well-known bit of footage in 1965 by releasing a cover of it on his album, wittily titled Best Of The Beatles.

Although the bulk of the songs were written by others (this was their chance to play those songs by as Elvis Presley, Little Richard, Chuck Berry and Buddy Holly that had inspired them so much), it did include one Lennon-McCartney original that had only previously been recorded and released by another artist: 'I'll Be On My Way' by Billy J. Kramer With The Dakotas. And of the compositions that had previously appeared as George Martin produced (Norman Smith engineered) singles and long players, it was interesting to hear them in less-polished form, as the *BBC* sessions didn't really allow for multiple takes or multi-track recordings. Sure, there is the occasional, "Yeah, that lick sounds even better than on the record...", but not that many.

'A Hard Day's Night' is far more stripped down, and has a far less jarring intro chord, but it does feature Harrison's un-faded coda. Also of note is the fact that Chuck Berry's 'Carol' was broadcast before the Rolling Stones covered it on their first album in 1964 and the fact that Lennon takes the lead on Carl Perkins' 'Honey Don't', whereas Starr sang it on *Beatles For Sale* and the version that later appeared on On Air – *Live At The BBC Volume 2.*

In November 2013, a remastered and repackaged version was issued to tie-in with the second volume. This featured some minor changes to the track listing and editing, as well as improved sound quality throughout. The sole musical addition was a version of 'From Us To You' at the end of the second disc.

BABY IT'S YOU

UK Release: Apple (Parlophone) R 6406, 20 March 1995 (EP)
US Release: Apple (Capitol) NR 7243 8 58348 1 3, 4 April 1995 (EP)
Recording data: 1 June 1963 - 17 November 1964, London
Producer: George Martin
Engineer: Terry Henebery, Bernie Andrews
Tracks: Baby It's You / I'll Follow The Sun / Devil In Her Heart / Boys

---

Their first UK single for 13 years, and the first to include previously unreleased recordings for 25. Yes, while the lead track appears on the *Live At The BBC* album, the other three - also from the Beeb's archives - do not (although two would be scooped-up for *On Air – Live At The BBC Volume 2* eighteen years later).

Having said that, there's not a lot to distinguish any of these recordings from those originally released and recorded by the band in 1963-64.

ANTHOLOGY 1

UK Release: Apple (Parlophone) CDPCSP 727, 21 November 1995 (LP)
US Release: Apple (Capitol) CDP 7243 8 34445 2 6, 21 November 1995 (LP)
Recording data: 1958 - 1994, London and elsewhere
Produced and directed by: George Martin
Remix Engineer: Geoff Emerick
Tracks: Free As A Bird / "We Were Four Guys...That's All" / That'll Be The Day / In Spite Of All The Danger / "Sometimes I'd Borrow...Those Still Exist" / Hallelujah, I Love Her So / You'll Be Mine / Cayenne / "First Of All...It Didn't Do A Thing Here" / My Bonnie / Ain't She Sweet? / Cry For A Shadow / "Brian Was A Beautiful Guy...He Presented Us Well" / "I Secured Them...A Beatle Drink Even Then" / Searchin' / Three Cool Cats / The Sheik Of Araby / Like Dreamers Do / Hello Little Girl / "Well, The Recording Test...By My Artists" / Besame Mucho / Love Me Do / How Do You Do It? / Please, Please Me / One After 909 (Sequence) / One After 909 (Complete) / Lend Me Your Comb / I'll Get You / "We Were Performers...In Britain" / I Saw Her Standing There / From Me To You / Money (That's What I Want) / You Really Got A Hold On Me / Roll Over Beethoven / She Loves You / Till There Was You / Twist And Shout / This Boy / I Want To Hold Your Hand / "Boys, What I Was Thinking..." / Moonlight Bay / Can't Buy Me Love / All My Loving / You Can't Do That / And I Love Her / A Hard Day's Night / I Wanna Be Your Man / Long Tall Sally / Boys / Shout / I'll Be Back (Demo) / I'll Be Back (Complete) / You Know What To Do / No Reply (Demo) / Mr. Moonlight / Leave My Kitten Alone / No Reply / Eight Days A Week (Sequence) / Eight Days A Week / Medley: Kansas City-Hey, Hey, Hey, Hey!

"I am trying to tell the story of the Beatles lives in music, from the moment they met to the moment they split up in 1970. I have listened to everything we ever recorded together. Every take of every song. Every track of every song, virtually everything that was ever committed to tape and labelled 'Beatles'. " **– George Martin**

Stories of a definitive Beatles' documentary, to be called *The Long And Winding Road*, had circulated for many years. But it wasn't until the early 90s that the project was formally announced, after years of to-ing and fro-ing. Harrison insisted it not be named after a McCartney song, and so Anthology was born.

As well as a TV series, *Anthology* also heralded a book ("The Beatles' story told for the first time in their own words and pictures") and the liberation of previously unheard music from *EMI's* archives. Producer Martin was to initially declare much of the band's unreleased material as "junk", and even McCartney joked on the release of this here volume one that he and Harrison were thinking of calling the next album "Scraping the bottom of the barrel". But in reality, *Anthology* contains copious slices of fried gold.

Opening with 'the first new Beatles song in 25 years', 'Free As A Bird', before going back to the beginning and the first recordings of The Quarrymen – featuring Lennon, McCartney and Harrison, with pianist John Lowe and drummer Colin Hanton – from 1958. 'In Spite Of All The Danger' was uniquely labelled a McCartney/Harrison composition, though the former would later decry the latter's contribution as merely "playing the guitar solo."

'Hello Little Girl' was the first song Lennon ever wrote and presented to the band. It appeared on their unsuccessful *Decca* audition tape, but they ended up giving it away to the Fourmost, whose 1963 recording (produced by George Martin at Abbey Road) reached number 9 in the UK charts.

There are performances from live shows and TV appearances (like the 1963 Royal Command Performance where Lennon made his famous "rattle your jewellery" quip, and with the legendary comic duo Morecambe And Wise), as well as parts of their *Decca* audition tape and the recordings with Bert Kaempfert in Hamburg.

But it's the *EMI* studio recordings that hold most of the appeal. An early take of 'Can't Buy Me Love' has backing vocal harmonies by Lennon and Harrison that were quickly dropped as a bad idea. Similarly, the more up-tempo Mersey-beat arrangement of 'And I Love Her' was mercifully reworked for its original release.

On some songs you get excerpts from different takes side by side, showing you how the band quickly changed the beat or arrangement for the better – like on 'I'll Be Back'. Elsewhere, you get false starts, giggles and composite performances made from incomplete or botched takes (like 'One After 909').

Their version of Little Willie John's 'Leave My Kitten Alone' was finished to their satisfaction in 1964 and intended for the *Beatles For Sale* album, but never made it. There were rumours of a likely release for years (including as a single in the early 1980s, backed with the 1963 recording of 'One After 909') before it finally appeared here.

This album was released on the day that Led Zeppelin's former manager, Peter Grant, suffered a fatal heart attack.

FREE AS A BIRD / CHRISTMAS TIME (IS HERE AGAIN)

UK Release: Apple (Parlophone) R 6422, 4 December 1995 (SP)
US Release: Apple (Capitol) NR 58497, 12 December 1995 (SP)
Recording data: 1963, 1967, 1977 & 1994, London, New York and Sussex.
Producer: Jeff Lynne
Engineer: Geoff Emerick
Additional tracks on CD single: I Saw Her Standing There / This Boy

---

"We took the attitude that John had gone on holiday, saying 'I finished all the tracks except this one but I leave it to you guys to finish it off.'" – **Paul McCartney**

Released as part of the promotion for the Anthology project, 'Free As A Bird' is a song based around a home demo written and recorded by Lennon in 1977, which the other three overdubbed, wrote extra words for and generally re-arranged in 1994.

Although Lynne strived to ensure this (and the next single, 'Real Love') sounded like the old Beatles, Harrison commented at the time that "It sounds like them now," perhaps because of his prominent slide guitar, which was more reminiscent of his post-Beatles solo work. Of course, Lynne had also co-produced his platinum selling Cloud Nine album in 1987, and was a part of Harrison's subsequent supergroup – along with Roy Orbison, Bob Dylan and Tom Petty – McBusted... er, I mean the Traveling Wilburys.

A music video was created for 'Free As A Bird', directed by Joe Pytka. This included numerous references to Beatles songs, and was premiered on UK TV in November 1995 when the six-part *Anthology* documentary series was first shown.

The song ends with Harrison strumming a ukulele with a backward recording of Lennon saying "Turned out nice again!" This was the catchphrase of the late British comedy actor/singer-songwriter George Formby, of whom Harrison in particular was a huge fan.

The cover for the single features a drawing by Lennon that first appeared in In His Own Write in 1964. 'Free As A Bird' won the 1997 Grammy Award for Best Pop Performance By A Duo Or Group With Vocal.

As per the live at the *BBC* 'Baby It's You' EP, the CD single included three tracks not on the preceding album.

'Christmas Time (Is Here Again)' was largely extracted from the Beatles' 1967 Christmas fan club single, though a smidge of dialogue from the previous year's flexi disc was added at the end. Starr later recorded a solo version of the song for his 1999 album, 'I Wanna Be Santa Claus'. 'I Saw Her Standing There' and 'This Boy' are *EMI* studio outtakes.

Released on 4 December, eh? Not a great day, what with the Montreux Casino in Switzerland being set ablaze during a Frank Zappa & The Mothers concert that day (in 1971 - we know a song about that, right?) and Led Zeppelin officially disbanding following the death of drummer John Bonham (in 1980). It was also the day that Zappa succumbed to prostate cancer in 1993. And the actual day that Zeppelin's manager Peter Grant was buried. On a brighter note, it's Jeff Bridges birthday. The dude abides.

REAL LOVE / BABY'S IN BLACK

UK Release: Apple (Parlophone) R 6425, 4 March 1996 (SP)
US Release: Apple (Capitol) NR 58544, 5 March 1996 (SP)
Recording data: 1965, 1966, 1980 & 1995, Los Angeles, London, Bermuda and Sussex.
Producer: Jeff Lynne
Engineer: Geoff Emerick, Jon Jacobs
Additional tracks on CD single: Yellow Submarine / Here, There And Everywhere

---

"I had to get rid of the hiss and the mains hum, and then there were clicks all the way through it. We'd spend a day on it, then listen back and still find loads more things wrong. It didn't have any effect on John's voice, because we were just dealing with the air surrounding him, in between phrases. That took about a week to clean up before it was even usable. Putting fresh music to it was the easy part." **– Jeff Lynne**

Released as a trailer for the *Anthology 2* album. Although Martin was credited as producer/director of all three volumes, he was not involved in the production of two new songs created for the first two; at the time, McCartney said, "George doesn't want to produce much anymore 'cause his hearing's not as good as it used to be. He's a very sensible guy, and he says, 'Look, Paul I like to do a proper job', and if he doesn't feel he's up to it he won't do it. It's very noble of him, actually — most people would take the money and run."

Once again, a Lennon demo tweaked by the others many years later. Unlike 'Free As A Bird', however, Lennon's original recording and arrangement of the piece was far more complete - indeed, unbeknownst to McCartney, a solo version of 'Real Love' had already been issued as part of the soundtrack to the documentary film, Imagine: John Lennon in October 1988 - although this was an alternate take.

Also as per 'Free As A Bird', the CD single included a further three tracks not included on the Anthology albums. 'Baby's In Black' was recorded live at the Hollywood Bowl in August 1965, and features a typically droll intro by Lennon. 'Yellow Submarine' similarly has a spoken intro - this time by Starr, over the sound of marching charging feet, boy. The song has also been newly remixed to place emphasis on the myriad sound effects employed. Likewise, 'Here, There And Everywhere' sports a 1995 remix of the lads' lush vocal harmonies overdubbed onto an alternative take of this other *Revolver* song.

The single was released a week before Thomas Hamilton shot 16 infant school children and one teacher at the Dunblane Primary School in Scotland.

ANTHOLOGY 2

UK Release: Apple (Parlophone) CDPCSP 728, 18 March 1996 (LP)
US Release: Apple (Capitol) CDP 7243 8 34448 2 3, 19 March 1996 (LP)
Recording data: 1965 – 1994, London and elsewhere.
Produced and directed by: George Martin
Remix Engineer: Geoff Emerick

Tracks: Real Love / Yes It Is (Takes 2 & 14) / I'm Down (Take 1) / You've Got To Hide Your Love Away (Takes 1, 2 & 5) / If You've Got Trouble (Take 1) / That Means A Lot / Yesterday (Take 1) / It's Only Love (Takes 2 & 3) / I Feel Fine / Ticket To Ride / Yesterday / Help! / Everybody's Trying To Be My Baby / Norwegian Wood (This Bird Has Flown) (Take 1) / I'm Looking Through You (Take 1) / 12-Bar Original (Edited Take 2) / Tomorrow Never Knows (Take 1) / Got To Get You Into My Life (Take 5) / And Your Bird Can Sing (Take 2) / Taxman (Take 11) / Eleanor Rigby (Take 14) / I'm Only Sleeping (Rehearsal) / I'm Only Sleeping (Take 1) / Rock And Roll Music / She's A Woman / Strawberry Fields Forever (Demo Sequence) / Strawberry Fields Forever (Take 1) / Strawberry Fields Forever (Take 7 & Edit Piece) / Penny Lane (Take 9 Horn Overdub) / A Day In The Life (Takes 1, 2, 6 & Orchestra) / Good Morning Good Morning (Take 8) / Only A Northern Song (Takes 3 & 12) / Being For The Benefit Of Mr. Kite! (Takes 1 & 2) / Being For The Benefit Of Mr. Kite! (Take 7 & Effects Tape) / Lucy In The Sky With Diamonds (Takes 6, 7 & 8) / Within You Without You / Sgt. Pepper's Lonely Hearts Club Band (Reprise) (Take 5) / You Know My Name (Look Up The Number) / I Am The Walrus (Take 16) / The Fool On The Hill / Your Mother Should Know (Take 27) / The Fool On The Hill / Hello, Goodbye (Take 16 And Overdubs) / Lady Madonna (Takes 3 & 4) / Across The Universe (Take 2)

If newcomers to the Beatles bought this having heard 'Real Love' and jumped straight to track two, they'd probably be horrified thinking they'd wasted their coffers. The version of 'Yes It Is' here is, like much of *Anthology*, of greater interest to the more hard-core fan. Fortunately, the surprising inclusion of Lennon's unsteady guide vocal is about the closest they ever came to what Charles Montgomery Burns once described as their off-key caterwauling.

But disc one of this second Anthology volume gets much better with the inclusion of a studio version of 'Yesterday' by McCartney alone (there's also a live rendition where he's accompanied by strings and screams), 'Got To Get You Into My Life' without the brass, a vocal less 'strings only' performance of 'Eleanor Rigby' and 'And Your Bird Can Sing' sung by its two stoned/giggling composers.

'If You've Got Trouble' and 'That Means A Lot' were songs recorded during the *Help!* sessions, but both were vetoed: the former was to have been the album's 'Ringo song', while the latter was given away to P.J. Proby as someone who could do it greater justice. 'Norwegian Wood' signals something of a step change: they spent a lot of time producing this particular rendition, and it would have made the *Rubber Soul* album... had they not decided to completely re-record it nine days later. Fast disappearing were the days when they perfected an arrangement on the road and were able to record it quickly in the studio. The same applies to 'I'm Looking Through You', which here lacks its "Why, tell me why" choruses.

And this version of 'Taxman' replaces the "Mister Wilson, Mister Heath" line with "anybody got a bit of money?".

They clearly knew when they had winning material (unlike the rejected *Help!* songs), and all of these refinements certainly enhance the versions now familiar to millions.

At the start of disc two we hear the various changes made to the arrangement of 'Strawberry Fields Forever', pieced together before our very ears from solo Lennon demo to final sublime studio madness.

Elsewhere, 'A Day In The Life', 'Lucy In The Sky With Diamonds' and 'Lady Madonna' utilise the best outtakes from the songs' recordings stitched together and remixed specifically for this album

The instrumental backing track to Harrison's Pepper raga 'Within You Without You' is included as well, along with the unedited version of the original lunacy that is 'You Know My Name (Look Up The Number)', in stereo for the first time.

And 'I Am The Walrus' is the basic master minus string overdubs and the effects that make it that extra bit special.

Clearly a little more subsequent studio tinkerment went into creating this volume, but it does cover the period when the studio was the then unified band's playground. Accordingly, it is probably the best of the three volumes.

This album was released the day a fire at the Ozone Disco Club in Quezon City killed 162 people - the worst fire in Philippine history. One would hope that Mr Harrison did not see this as further cause for celebration.

ANTHOLOGY 3

UK Release: Apple (Parlophone) CDPCSP 729, 28 October 1996 (LP)
US Release: Apple (Capitol) CDP 7243 8 34451 2 7, 29 October 1996 (LP)
Recording data: May 1968 – January 1970, London and Esher.
Produced and directed by: George Martin
Remix Engineer: Geoff Emerick
Tracks: A Beginning / Happiness Is A Warm Gun / Helter Skelter / Mean Mr Mustard / Polythene Pam / Glass Onion / Junk / Piggies / Honey Pie / Don't Pass Me By / Ob-La-Di Ob-La-Da / Good Night / Cry Baby Cry / Blackbird / Sexy Sadie / While My Guitar Gently Weeps / Hey Jude / Not Guilty / Mother Nature's Son / Glass Onion / Rocky Raccoon / What's The New Mary Jane / Step Inside Love-Los Paranoias / I'm So Tired / I Will / Why Don't We Do It In The Road / Julia / I've Got A Feeling / She Came In Through The Bathroom Window / Dig A Pony / Two Of Us / For You Blue / Teddy Boy / Medley: Rip It Up-Shake, Rattle and Roll-Blue Suede Shoes / The Long And Winding Road / Oh! Darling / All Things Must Pass / Mailman, Bring Me No More Blues /Get Back / Old Brown Shoe / Octopus's Garden / Maxwell's Silver Hammer / Something / Come Together / Come And Get It / Ain't She Sweet / Because / Let It Be / I Me Mine / The End

---

With no third 'new' single, this album kicks off with a short flute-led orchestral piece recorded by the musicians on 'Good Night' and meant by Martin as an introduction to Starr's 'Don't Pass Me By'. The whole first disc is from 1968 and revolves around "White Album" material, with 'Happiness Is A Warm Gun' the first of seven Kinfauns demos, all licensed to *Apple* by Harrison (the others being 'Mean Mr. Mustard', 'Polythene Pam', 'Glass Onion', 'Junk', 'Piggies' and 'Honey Pie', all captured on his Ampex 4-track).

'Not Guilty' and 'What's The New Mary Jane' were both long known about (and bootlegged) recordings for which room could not be found on "The White Album". Harrison would later re-record a far more chilled version of 'Not Guilty' for his eponymous sixth solo album, but this band version is a lot more dissonant, and all the better for it.

Lennon's 'What's The New Mary Jane' was likely a step too far, with Lennon clearly lobbying harder for 'Revolution 9' to be included on the album. Featuring piano, bells, various sound effects and wailing from Ono, Lennon, Harrison and roadie Evans, it ends with its creator saying, "Let's hear it...before we get taken away!" Remember, this was the man who once famously declared "avant-garde is French for bullshit". When I first heard it (in the 70s – a friend lent me a bootleg with it on, honest), I found it a bit creepy. But now I love it. Stop the clocks, I'm ready for 'Carnival Of Light'!

Some are quick to dismiss this disorderly druggy dirge, but the lyrics are actually quite witty and it clearly wasn't just Lennon making it up as he went along; they attempted four recordings at *EMI*, and it had earlier been demoed at Kinfauns. This was the final and longest take.

The first disc also includes a lovely solo take of McCartney perfecting 'Mother Nature's Son'.

Onto the second disc, and (with the exception of 'I Me Mine') it's all from 1969 and sessions for *Get Back/Let It Be/Abbey Road*. The medley of old rock and roll tunes, their charming take on Buddy Holly's 'Mailman, Bring Me No More Blues' and 'Ain't She Sweet', represents their default fallback option when things were getting too tense while trying to work on their own self-penned material. You can hear Lennon taking the piss with barn dance calls during McCartney's run-through of 'Teddy Boy', which can't have helped. McCartney would abandon the songs until after the band broke up and (like his song 'Junk') recorded anew and released it on his debut solo album – issued a month ahead of *Let It Be*, much to the chagrin of the other three.

Lennon more successfuly hijacks 'Oh! Darling', with the news that Ono's divorce "has just gone through".

Another song that would later appear on a post-Beatles solo album was Harrison's

'All Things Must Pass' – in fact, it became the title of his hugely successful third solo album (as well as Wonderwall, Harrison released the experimental *Electronic Sound* album before the band's 'legal separation'). The demo here was recorded on his 26th birthday.

Not included though is a demo version of Harrison's 'Isn't It a Pity', correspondingly recorded during the *Get Back* sessions. This was made available on the 'best of' album, Let It Roll: Songs By George Harrison, as an *iTunes* Store exclusive in 2009.

McCartney's multi-tracked solo demo of 'Come And Get It' is almost identical to the version he produced for *Apple* signing The Iveys, who had a top five hit with it in early 1970 – the group by then having renamed themselves Badfinger.

For me, the highlight of this set is the a capella rendering of the *Abbey Road* song, 'Because'. Remixed for this volume, the spine-tingling harmonics of Lennon, McCartney and Harrison shine bright, making it sound like they're standing on the shoulder of giants.

The album ends with a new remix of the last song performed by the whole band on the Beatles' last recorded album.

The end.

With this third volume, buyers could finally line the discs up and gaze in wonder at the full magnificence of the from-Liverpool-to-Let-It-Be collage painted by Voormann and fellow artist, Alfons Kiefer.

Anthology 3 was released five days into the civil trial of retired American footballer/actor, O.J. Simpson, which would find him liable for the wrongful death of Ronald Goldman and the battery of Nicole Brown. Well, if the glove fits...

YELLOW SUBMARINE SONGTRACK

UK Release: Apple (Parlophone) 521 4812, 13 September 1999 (LP)
US: Apple (Capitol) CDP 7243 5 21481 2 7, 17 September 1999 (LP)
Recording data: 1965–1968 at EMI, Olympic and De Lane Lea studios, London
Producer: George Martin
Remix engineer: Peter Cobbin assisted by Paul Hicks and Mirek Stiles
Tracks: Yellow Submarine / Hey Bulldog / Eleanor Rigby / Love You To / All Together Now / Lucy In The Sky With Diamonds / Think For Yourself / Sgt. Pepper's Lonely Hearts Club Band / With A Little Help From My Friends / Baby, You're A Rich Man / Only A Northern Song / All You Need Is Love / When I'm Sixty-Four / Nowhere Man / It's All Too Much

---

Released to coincide with the 1999 home video re-release of the restored *Yellow Submarine* film, an album of only the Beatles songs heard in the film (with the exception of 'I Am The Walrus' and 'A Day In The Life') for those who can't be arsed to wade through Martin's orchestral score.

Unlike other Beatles remasters, the songs were fully remixed from the original multi-track tapes – something that has not been done for any of the CD releases of the core catalogue with the exception of *Help!* and *Rubber Soul* (the 1965 stereo mixes of which Martin thought were "very woolly" and so prepared digital remixes in 1986).

Although remixed, the songs on the *Yellow Submarine Songtrack* remain the previously available standard catalogue recordings - they just sound a whole lot better.

1

UK Release: Apple 529 9702, 13 November 2000 (LP)
Recording data: 11 September 1962 - 1 April 1970, EMI, Apple, Olympic and Trident Studios, London; Pathé Marconi Studios, Paris
Producer: George Martin, Phil Spector
Remastering engineer: Peter Mew
Tracks: Love Me Do / From Me To You / She Loves You / I Want To Hold Your Hand / Can't Buy Me Love / A Hard Day's Night / I Feel Fine / Eight Days A Week / Ticket To Ride / Help! / Yesterday / Day Tripper / We Can Work It Out / Paperback Writer / Yellow Submarine / Eleanor Rigby / Penny Lane / All You Need Is Love / Hello, Goodbye / Lady Madonna / Hey Jude / Get Back / The Ballad Of John And Yoko / Something / Come Together / Let It Be / The Long And Winding Road

---

An album of virtually every number one single released in the UK and US from 1962 to 1970 - in chronological order – compiled by Messrs Harrison, Martin, McCartney and Starr. Issued on the 30th anniversary of the band's break-up, it went to number 1 worldwide – the first time a Beatles compilation had ever reached the top of the charts in the UK. So not as pointless as I personally thought (especially after the *20 Greatest Hits* albums). And a clear inspiration to record company executives, who followed this with the hugely successful *ELV1S* and *Bee Gees' Number Ones* collections.

LET IT BE... NAKED

UK Release: Apple (Parlophone) 595 7132, 17 November 2003 (LP)
Recording data: February 1968, January–February 1969, January and March–April 1970, EMI and Apple studios and Twickenham Film Studios, London
Producer: Paul Hicks, Guy Massey and Allan Rouse
Original Engineer: Glyn Johns
Tracks: Get Back / Dig a Pony / For You Blue / The Long and Winding Road / Two Of Us / I've Got A Feeling / One After 909 / Don't Let Me Down / I Me Mine / Across The Universe / Let It Be.
Fly On The Wall bonus disc: Sun King / Don't Let Me Down / One After 909 / Because I Know You Love Me So / Don't Pass Me By / Taking a Trip to Carolina / John's Piano Piece / Child Of Nature / Back In The U.S.S.R. / Every Little Thing / Don't Let Me Down / All Things Must Pass / John's Jam / She Came In Through The Bathroom Window / Paul's Bass Jam / Paul's Piano Piece / Get Back / Two Of Us / Maggie Mae / Fancy My Chances With You / Can You Dig It? / Get Back

---

"If we'd had today's technology back then, it would sound like this because this is the noise we made in the studio. It's all exactly as it was in the room. You're right there now."
– Paul McCartney

A remixed and edited version of the original *Let It Be* album, ostensibly cobbled together by McCartney, who was never whelmed with the orchestral and choral overdubs later added by Phil Spector.

The original intent was that this 'stripped down' version would complement a DVD release of the *Let It Be* documentary film. At the time of writing, this has still to happen - with the film officially unavailable now since the 80s.

This album was released the day before the Local Government Act 2003 became effective. This Act repealed the controversial amendment Section 28, introduced by the Thatcher Government in the 1980s, which stated that a local authority "shall not intentionally promote homosexuality or publish material with the intention of promoting homosexuality." Gone. Good riddance.

LOVE

UK Release: Apple (Parlophone) 3798082 / Apple (Parlophone) 3798102 (with DVD-Audio), 20 November 2006 (LP)
US Release: Apple (Capitol) 0946 3 79808 2 8/ Apple (Capitol) 0946 3 79810 2 3 (with DVD-Audio), 21 November 2006 (LP)
Recording data: 1963–1969 at EMI, Trident, Olympic and Apple studios, London, EMI Studios, Bombay and Hollywood Bowl, Los Angeles; mixed 2004-2006 at Abbey Road Studios
Producer: George Martin, Giles Martin
Remix engineer: Paul Hicks
Tracks: Because / Get Back / Glass Onion / Eleanor Rigby (with Julia Transition) / I Am The Walrus / I Want To Hold Your Hand / Drive My Car-The Word-What You're Doing / Gnik Nus / Something (with Blue Jay Way Transition) / Being For The Benefit Of Mr. Kite!-I Want You (She's So Heavy)-Helter Skelter / Help! / Blackbird-Yesterday / Strawberry Fields Forever / Within You Without You-Tomorrow Never Knows / Lucy In The Sky With Diamonds / Octopus's Garden / Lady Madonna / Here Comes The Sun (with The Inner Light Transition) / Come Together-Dear Prudence (with Cry Baby Cry Transition) / Revolution / Back In The U.S.S.R. / While My Guitar Gently Weeps / A Day In The Life / Hey Jude / Sgt. Pepper's Lonely Hearts Club Band (Reprise) / All You Need Is Love
iTunes Exclusive bonus tracks: The Fool On The Hill / Girl

"What people will be hearing on the album is a new experience, a way of re-living the whole Beatles musical lifespan in a very condensed period." **– Giles Martin**

Aside from *Past Masters*, possibly the only truly worthwhile Beatles compilation of extant material. The Martin's mash-up of 130 snippets from commercially released and demo recordings by The Beatles for the Cirque du Soleil's Las Vegas show is a real winner. Put your headphones on and get adrift on memory bliss.

The way they combine the vocals and sitar from 'Within You Without You' with the bass and drums from 'Tomorrow Never Knows' is just one of many highlights. Dialogue from The Beatles' third and fourth fan-club Christmas Records (1965 and 1966) is featured towards the end of the album.

The *iTunes* rendering – released in 2011 - contains two previously unreleased versions of two complete songs plus, like the DVD-Audio edition, slightly longer versions of both 'Revolution' and 'Back In The U.S.S.R'.

THE BEATLES STEREO BOX SET

UK/US Release: Apple 5099969944901, 9 September 2009 (LP)
Recording data: 1962–1970, at EMI, Trident, Olympic, Apple, De Lane Lea, Chappell and Regent Sound studios, London; Pathé Marconi Studio, Paris; EMI Studios, Bombay.
Producer: George Martin
Remastering engineers: Guy Massey, Paul Hicks, Sam Okell, Sean Magee, Steve Rooke
Albums: Please Please Me / With The Beatles / A Hard Day's Night / Beatles for Sale / Help! / Rubber Soul / Revolver / Sgt. Pepper's Lonely Hearts Club Band / Magical Mystery Tour / The Beatles / Yellow Submarine / Abbey Road / Let It Be / Past Masters

---

A box set consisting of all the 2009 remastered stereo albums. The remastering project was led by *EMI* senior studio engineers Allan Rouse and Guy Massey. The set also includes a DVD containing all of the short films that are on the individual CDs issued the same day in QuickTime format.

THE BEATLES IN MONO

UK/US Release: Apple 5099969945120, 9 September 2009 (LP)
Recording data: 1962–1970 at EMI, Trident, Olympic, Apple, Chappell, De Lane Lea and Regent Sound studios, London; Pathé Marconi Studio, Paris; EMI Studios, Bombay
Producer: George Martin
Remastering engineers: Guy Massey, Paul Hicks, Sean Magee, Steve Rooke
Albums: Please Please Me / With The Beatles / A Hard Day's Night / Beatles for Sale / Help! / Rubber Soul / Revolver / Sgt. Pepper's Lonely Hearts Club Band / Magical Mystery Tour / The Beatles / Mono Masters

---

"At that time the console was about this big with four faders on it. And there was one speaker right in the middle and that was it. When they invented stereo, I remember thinking 'Why? What do you want two speakers for?', because it ruined the sound from our point of view. You know, we had everything coming out of one speaker; now it had to come out of two speakers." – **George Harrison**

A box set consisting of all the remastered monophonic recordings made by the Beatles, which thus excludes *Yellow Submarine*, *Abbey Road* and *Let It Be*.

The mono box was released the same day as the stereo set to highlight the fact that the bulk of their catalogue was originally heard by the band - and released - in mono; the stereo mixes were largely created afterwards without their involvement.

Mono Masters is similar to the *Past Masters* double album, but the second disc replaces 'Old Brown Shoe', 'The Ballad Of John And Yoko' and 'Let It Be' with the five songs prepared in mono for the abandoned *Yellow Submarine* EP ('Only A Northern Song', 'All Together Now', 'Hey Bulldog', 'It's All Too Much' and 'Across The Universe'), all released here for the first time.

ANTHOLOGY HIGHLIGHTS

iTunes Store Release: EMI (Apple Records), 16 November 2010 (DD)
Recording data: 1963 – 1995, London and Sussex
Producer: George Martin
Remix Engineer: Geoff Emerick
Tracks: Free As A Bird / One After 909 (Complete) / That Means A Lot / Leave My Kitten Alone / If You've Got Trouble / Can't Buy Me Love / Mr. Moonlight / Medley: Kansas City-Hey, Hey, Hey, Hey! / Eight Days A Week (Complete) / I'm Looking Through You / Yesterday / Tomorrow Never Knows / Strawberry Fields Forever (Take 1) / Across The Universe / Something / Not Guilty / Octopus's Garden / All Things Must Pass / Come And Get It / Good Night / While My Guitar Gently Weeps / The Long And Winding Road / Real Love

---

An *iTunes*-only 'best of' . Some obvious choices (the two new singles, 'Come And Get It', 'Leave My Kitten Alone', and the complete 'One After 909') as well as some surprising ones ('Mr. Moonlight').

TOMORROW NEVER KNOWS

iTunes Store Release: EMI (Apple Records), 24 July 2012 (DD)
Recording data: 1964 – 1969, EMI Studios, London
Producer: George Martin
Engineers: Norman Smith, Geoff Emerick
Tracks: Revolution / Paperback Writer / And Your Bird Can Sing / Helter Skelter / Savoy Truffle / I'm Down / I've Got A Feeling / Back In The U.S.S.R. / You Can't Do That / It's All Too Much / She Said She Said / Hey Bulldog / Tomorrow Never Knows / The End

---

An officially sanctioned *iTunes*-only collection of the band's songs "that rock the hardest". Clearly this conflicts with the view of Bhaskar Menon, the president of *Capitol Records*, who put together the mid-70s *Rock 'N' Roll Music* compilation, as half the tracks here failed to make that earlier official release.

'I've Got A Feeling' and 'The End' are the *Let It Be... Naked* and *Anthology 3* versions. Otherwise, it's the more-familiar originals.

ON AIR - LIVE AT THE BBC VOLUME 2

UK Release: Apple (Parlophone) 3749169, 11 November 2013 (LP)
US Release: Apple (Capitol) B0019415-02, 11 November 2013 (LP)
Recording data: 1963 – 1966, United Kingdom – London, mainly.
Producers: Terry Henebery, Ian Grant, Peter Pilbeam, Jimmy Grant, Bernie Andrews, Ron Belchier, Bryant Marriott, Pete Dauncey, Brian Willey
Remastering Engineers: Guy Massey, Alex Wharton
Executive Producers: Kevin Howlett, Mike Heatley, Jeff Jones
Tracks: "And Here We Are Again" / Words Of Love / "How About It, Gorgeous?" / Do You Want To Know A Secret / Lucille / "Hey, Paul..." / Anna (Go To Him) / "Hello!" / Please Please Me / Misery / I'm Talking About You / "A Real Treat" / Boys / "Absolutely Fab" / Chains / Ask Me Why / Till There Was You / Lend Me Your Comb / "Lower 5E" / The Hippy Hippy Shake / Roll Over Beethoven / There's A Place / "Bumper Bundle" / P.S. I Love You / Beautiful Dreamer / Devil In Her Heart / "The 49 Weeks" / Sure To Fall (In Love With You) / "Never Mind, Eh?" / Twist And Shout / "Bye, Bye" / "John - Pop Profile" / "George - Pop Profile" / I Saw Her Standing There / Glad All Over/ "Lift Lid Again" / I'll Get You / She Loves You / Memphis, Tennessee / Happy Birthday Dear Saturday Club / "Now Hush, Hush" / From Me To You / Money (That's What I Want) / I Want To Hold Your Hand / "Brian Bathtubes" / This Boy / "If I Wasn't In America" / I Got A Woman / Long Tall Sally / If I Fell / "A Hard Job Writing Them" / And I Love Her / "Oh, Can't We? Yes We Can" / You Can't Do That / Honey Don't / I'll Follow The Sun / "Green With Black Shutters" / Medley: Kansas City-Hey, Hey, Hey, Hey! / "That's What We're Here For" / I Feel Fine (Studio Outtake) / "Paul - Pop Profile" / "Ringo - Pop Profile"

"There's a lot of energy and spirit. We are going for it, not holding back at all, trying to put in the best performance of our lifetimes." – **Paul McCartney**

Another for hard-cores, really. Only two 'new' songs (the rest largely re-recorded songs from their first four UK albums) and loads of relatively inane (or chuckle-at-just-the-once) between song chat. It's also a little annoying that the versions of 'Lend Me Your Comb', 'I'll Follow The Sun' and 'Boys' are the exact same one as on the first *Anthology* album and the Baby It's You EP. Given that they apparently recorded 'Boys' on seven occasions for the radio, should not one of those alternate takes be here now?

Where the first volume was edited so that the mix of music and dialogue made for a wondrously frenetic pace, this second batch is bogged down by a little too much chat. Don't believe the truth? Well Howlett (who has written books on the band's radio career) has stated that there is unlikely to be a third volume – they've exhausted all the good musical output. So we can only assume that means the boys singing 'Tie Me Kangaroo Down, Sport' with Rolf Harris will now never gain an official release.

Having said all that, the individual 'pop profile' interviews conducted by Brian Matthew in 1965/66 appended to the end of each side are a little more meaty. But as per Anthology, an *i-Tunes* highlights from volumes one and two might be prudent for the newbies.

The album was released the day before British composer John Tavener passed away - the day I actually got this album, in fact. Tavener's first recorded work, The Whale (a 'dramatic cantata', performed by the London Sinfonietta), was released on The Beatles' *Apple* label in 1970, largely thanks to Starr. Tavener's younger brother was doing some building work for Starr and clearly piqued his interest in his sibling. Lennon and Ono also became fans. Tavener later revealed that "Ringo is one of those shouting through a loud hailer in Melodrama & Pantomime on The Whale."

THE BEATLES BOOTLEG RECORDINGS 1963

iTunes Store Release: Universal Music Catalogue (Apple Records), 17 December 2013 (DD)
Recording data: 1963, London.
Producers: George Martin (studio outtakes), Terry Henebery, Ian Grant, Peter Pilbeam (BBC sessions)
Engineers: Norman Smith et al

Tracks: There's a Place (Takes 5 & 6) / There's a Place (Take 8) / There's a Place (Take 9) / Do You Want to Know a Secret (Track 2, Take 7) / A Taste of Honey (Track 2, Take 6) / I Saw Her Standing There (Take 2) / Misery (Take 1) / Misery (Take 7) / From Me to You (Takes 1 & 2) / From Me to You (Take 5) / Thank You Girl (Take 1) / Thank You Girl (Take 5) / One After 909 (Takes 1 & 2) / Hold Me Tight (Take 21) / Money (That's What I Want) (RM 7 Undubbed) / Some Other Guy (Live at the BBC for Saturday Club, 26 January 1963) / Love Me Do (Live at the BBC for Saturday Club, 26 January 1963) / Too Much Monkey Business (Live at the BBC for Saturday Club, 26 January 1963) / I Saw Her Standing There (Live at the BBC for Saturday Club, 16 March 1963) / Do You Want to Know a Secret (Live at the BBC for Saturday Club, 26 January 1963) / From Me to You (Live at the BBC for Saturday Club, 26 January 1963) / I Got to Find My Baby (Live at the BBC for Saturday Club, 26 January 1963) / Roll Over Beethoven (Live at the BBC for Saturday Club, 29 June 1963) / A Taste of Honey (Live at the BBC for Easy Beat, 23 June 1963) / Love Me Do (Live at the BBC for Easy Beat, 20 October 1963) / Please Please Me (Live at the BBC for Easy Beat, 20 October 1963) / She Loves You (Live at the BBC for Easy Beat, 20 October 1963) / I Want to Hold Your Hand (Live at the BBC for Saturday Club, 21 December 1963) / Till There Was You (Live at the BBC for Saturday Club, 21 December 1963) / Roll Over Beethoven (Live at the BBC for Saturday Club, 21 December 1963) / You Really Got a Hold on Me (Live at the BBC for Pop Go The Beatles, 4 June 1963) / The Hippy Hippy Shake (Live at the BBC for Pop Go The Beatles, 4 June 1963) / Till There Was You (Live at the BBC for Pop Go The Beatles, 11 June 1963) / A Shot of Rhythm and Blues (Live at the BBC for Pop Go The Beatles, 18 June 1963) / A Taste of Honey (Live at the BBC for Pop Go The Beatles, 18 June 1963) / Money (That's What I Want) (Live at the BBC for Pop Go The Beatles, 18 June 1963) / Anna (Go to Him) (Live at the BBC for Pop Go The Beatles, 25 June 1963) / Love Me Do (Live at the BBC for Pop Go The Beatles, 10 September 1963) / She Loves You (Live at the BBC for Pop Go The Beatles, 24 September 1963) / I'll Get You (Live at the BBC for Pop Go The Beatles, 10 September 1963) / A Taste of Honey (Live at the BBC for Pop Go The Beatles, 10 September 1963) / Boys (Live at the BBC for Pop Go The Beatles, 17 September 1963) / Chains (Live at the BBC for Pop Go The Beatles, 17 September 1963) / You Really Got a Hold on Me (Live at the BBC for Pop Go The Beatles, 17 September 1963) / I Saw Her Standing There (Live at the BBC for Pop Go The Beatles, 24 September 1963) / She Loves You (Live at the BBC for Pop Go The Beatles, 10 September 1963) / Twist and Shout (Live at the BBC for Pop Go The Beatles, 24 September 1963) / Do You Want to Know a Secret (Live at the BBC for Here We Go, 12 March 1963) / Please Please Me (Live at the BBC for Here We Go, 12 March 1963) / Long Tall Sally (Live at the BBC for Side by Side, 13 May 1963) / Chains (Live at the BBC for Side by Side, 13 May 1963) / Boys (Live at the BBC for Side by Side, 13 May 1963) / A Taste of Honey (Live at the BBC for Side by Side, 13 May 1963) / Roll Over Beethoven (Live at the BBC for From Us to You, 26 December 1963) / All My Loving (Live at the BBC for From Us to You, 26 December 1963) / She Loves You (Live at the BBC for From Us to You, 26 December 1963) / Till There Was You (Live at the BBC for From Us to You, 26 December 1963) / Bad To Me (Demo) / I'm In Love (Demo)

With very little fanfare, 59 recordings by The Beatles were exclusively released worldwide on *iTunes* on 17 December 2013 at a ridiculously exorbitant price - making a mockery of any claim to 'beat the boots'. This album was evidently released simply to prevent unreleased recordings made by the Beatles over fifty years ago from legally entering the public domain in Europe due to revised copyright laws. We can therefore expect another volume in each of the next few years.

Comprising more than two hours of studio outtakes, demos and yet further *BBC* recordings, it is still something of a curate's egg - its main redeeming features being the demo recordings of Lennon and McCartney's 'Bad To Me' (the song they bequeathed to Billy J. Kramer, you'll recall), and 'I'm In Love' (which the Fourmost recorded with George Martin at Abbey Road; Kramer also taped it, but the Fourmost's version was selected for release, becoming a minor UK hit at the end of 1963).

Appendix

THINGS WE SAID TODAY...

As will be noted elsewhere, I have also written a book for Wymer about the late great American composer Frank Zappa – specifically, one covering his final world tour of 1988. The one that ended in disarray. Buy a copy if you're unsure. Hell, buy a copy anyway.
At any rate, having previously written for the Zappa fanzine T'Mershi Duween, in the year of our Lord 2000 I started to run the UK's only website devoted to all things FZ. Having befriended a number of the musicians who worked with the man and his family, a year or so after the site's inception I asked a few of them to list their top ten songs by the Beatles. Hey, why not?

While I was writing this book, I decided to revisit this and asked a few more Zappa folk to contribute their thoughts. Let me introduce to you, some of the finest people talking about the finest band that ever there was.

WARREN CUCCURULLO (FZ, Missing Persons & Duran Duran guitarist): Definitely one of the most difficult top 10s you'd ever wanna do. For someone of my age (born 8 December 1956), who was interested in playing an instrument, the Beatles' music was an important and influential force. They opened up universes for the next generation of songwriters to come. They managed to change the course of popular music forever. (Positively, as opposed to new kids on the block, who've hopefully only changed the course for a few more minutes.) These songs here bring back many memories for me, and they sound just as good now as they ever did:

I Am The Walrus
Strawberry Fields Forever
A Day In The Life
Within You Without You
Happiness Is A Warm Gun
Helter Skelter
I Want You (She's So Heavy)
Dear Prudence
Help!
Everybody's Got Something To Hide Except Me And My Monkey

Jesus fuckin' Christ! I forgot 'Oh! Darling', 'Revolution' ...damn! It's impossible to pick through their stuff. I feel like a Nick Hornby character whose about to have a nervous breakdown. Thanks, it was fun. For future reference, 'The Idiot Bastard Son' is probably my number one FZ tune."...

*****

DON PRESTON (Mother & Grandmother): I'm sorry to say that I can't even think of 10 Beatles' songs. If I listened to the Beatles, I could give an evaluation but I don't have one Beatles' record. There are two songs that stick out in my mind – one is Penny Lane and the other (on the same album), which I can't recall the name but some words are "cu cu ca chub".

*****

PAMELA DES BARRES (GTO, groupie & author):

All You Need Is Love
We Can Work It Out
And I Love Her
Revolution 1
Eleanor Rigby
A Day In The Life
Got To Get You Into My Life
In My Life
Let It Be
Things We Said Today

Pamela first listed these ten tracks in an article in the UK music magazine Uncut, which inspired me to seek the views of other Zappa-related artists. Over ten years later, Pamela told me the list still stood and it would be okay to reprint it - adding that she is writing her own Beatles book! So keep 'em peeled for that one.

*****

MARK VOLMAN (Mother, Turtle & Phlorescent Leech): These are the songs that I would make a record out of. The Beatles are so much a part of the changes in my own life and each album had significance for me at its time of release:

It's All Too Much
Every Little Thing
Baby, You're a Rich Man
Here, There and Everywhere
Girl
The Night Before
What You're Doing
Getting Better
9. & 10. Tomorrow Never Knows; She Said She Said; I'm Only Sleeping; You Never Give Me Your Money; Dear Prudence; Two Of Us; Only A Northern Song; Hey Bulldog; It's Only Love; Drive My Car; If I Needed Someone; I'm Happy Just To Dance With You; Things We Said Today; In My Life; Within You Without You; I Will; Because; and so on and so on...
I purposely stayed away from singles. That would have to be another entire list. I have done a Beatles top-ten list before. I think the list was entirely different. I think the list changes depending on the mood you're in when asked. Each of them brought something to the group that I could not imagine not being there.

*****

JOE TRAVERS (Vaultmeister & former Zappa Plays Zappa drummer): Personal ten (in no specific order):

I Feel Fine
Getting Better
I've Got A Feeling

She Said She Said
You've Got To Hide Your Love Away
Revolution 9
Oh! Darling
Yer Blues
Blue Jay Way
If I Fell

There is just way too much mightiness going on with all of the Beatles. John by far is the heaviest of them all; such a potent songwriter, it's frightening. He would have to be number one. Paul comes next as the most talented. He plays all the necessary instruments well with a special unique quality that is undeniably him. And he also is an amazing songwriter. Number three will be Ringo, all because of his unbelievably special drum feel; the most appropriate drummer in the history of Rock & Roll. Everything he does is right. I had the pleasure of saying "Hi" to him and listened to him play drums through another room. It was unmistakingly him. I smiled. This was a couple of years ago.

*****

JIMMY CARL BLACK (original Mother, Grandmother, Muffin Man & Indian of the group): It's really hard to say which ones are my favourites because I love them all. I am a huge fan of John Lennon, but here goes:

I Am The Walrus
A Day In The Life
Blue Jay Way
Good Day Sunshine
The End
Come Together
Got To Get You Into My Life
In My Life
Lucy In The Sky With Diamonds
You Never Give Me Your Money

...and about a million more songs that are great.

*****

ARTHUR BARROW (FZ and Banned From Utopia bassist/Clonemeister): I love almost everything by the Beatles, so I don't think I could pick my top 3. I don't know how they did it – how they wrote so many great songs, how well their voices blended, the production, their sense of fun, just everything – it's almost scary.

*****

SCOTT THUNES (FZ, Dweezil Zappa, Steve Vai, Mother Hips bassist extraordinaire): Making a list of my favourite anything is tough enough, so I think I'll leave the Beatles action to the pros.

I always identified with George. He was cute in a rough way. He was the 'outsider' inside the band. The 'quiet' one. I liked that. His scene in *A Hard Day's Night* with the insolence directed at the clueless industry people seemed most like the way I'd like to conduct myself in that world. His guitar playing is what freaks me out though. I swear he never played a solo that didn't go 'sharp'. I always wondered about that. The 'best' guitarist in the world and nobody - including George Martin - could make him play in tune. Or they didn't want him to. Freaks me out.

*****

MIKE KENEALLY (FZ, Steve Vai, Beer For Dolphins & solo guitarist/keyboardist): Off the top of me head:

Dear Prudence – haunting, one of a kind.
I'm Looking Through You – perfect.
I've Just Seen A Face – happiness!
I Dig A Pony – it's just very cool.
No Reply – one of the best beginnings of an album ever (especially the too-heavily-reverbed 'Beatles '65' US version).
I'm A Loser – one of the best second songs on an album ever.
The Inner Light – really gorgeous and inspiring.
You Know My Name (Look Up The Number) – original 45 b-side version.
She Said She Said – prototypical Lennon odd-time psychedelic wonderfulness.
Rain – 'She Said She Said' Part two, but better. And I'm pretty sure that 'Rain' came out before 'She Said She Said', didn't it? All right, each one is phaze two of the other then. She Said She Said – 'Rain' Phaze Two; Rain – 'She Said She Said' Phaze Two.
We Can Work It Out – perfect.

That's eleven! That's too bad! (If you have to cut a song, make it 'Pony'.) Oh, and my favourite children's author is L. Frank Baum.

*****

CANDY ZAPPA (singing sister): Well let's see, my 10 favourite Beatles songs... hmm...

Yes It Is – when I was 13 and the Beatles came out, I was fascinated by them and this song was so sweet sounding, it melted me... imagine me melting. Oy vey...
Baby You Can Drive My Car – this song brought out the macho in me. Yeah, me driving
There's A Place – a tight harmonic blend that really got to me. Tight, yeah...
Honey Pie – a silly chauvinistic song that made me laugh.
Maxwell's Silver Hammer – a raucous visually violent ditty. And they let him in school??
Helter Skelter – a scary song...
I'm Only Sleeping – the only other thing I couldn't get enough of was sleep itself
This Boy – a confusing song, but after listening to it 30 or 40 million times, I got it...
I'll Follow The Sun – I remember one time I was listening to this song and singing along with it and Frank was listening to me sing and when it was over he said that it was a "kissy" song, I guess to him that was wimpy. Ha!
Julia – John's touching tribute to his mum... beautiful.

Will that do it, I hope? Love, Candy.

*****

THANA HARRIS (Queen of the Universe): Beatles songs... don't have ten, but I loved the Beatles because I turned 13 when they we're going more radical – late sixties. Overall favourites: Strawberry Fields Forever; Here Comes the Sun; Don't Let Me Down; Something; Let it Be; The Long And Winding Road. Solo album fave: Imagine. I still like the music and the poetry in these tunes. They were all soothing during hard times.

*****

ESSRA MOHAWK (one-time Mother, Uncle Meat, musician, songwriter): I think I've loved every Beatle song I've ever heard from the very beginning. I immediately heard their unique sound in that first record. It was either I Saw Her Standing There or I Want To Hold Your Hand. They both have that certain style, that vocal blend like nobody else's.

*****

ALBERT WING (FZ, Fowler Brothers, Shuggie Otis saxophonist): I was not an avid Beatles fan, though I did like their music.

*****

ROBERT MARTIN (FZ, Banned From Utopia hornist, saxophonist, keyboardist): Here's my list of favourite Beatles songs, listed alphabetically, as I find it impossible to rank them in terms of favouring one above another. It was supposed to be a top ten list, but there are just so many great Beatles songs that it's hard enough to narrow it down to these fourteen, let alone rank them.

And I Love Her - the melody in the verse blends haunting elements of Russian romanticism with a little middle Eastern flavour, and the tension it sets up resolves perfectly, like a sigh of relief, into "...and I love her."

Back In The U.S.S.R. - aside from the fact that it's a rockin' song, it showed great chutzpah to throw those lyrics out there at a time in world politics when it was bound to raise some eyebrows.

Come Together - an unusually swampy groove for the Beatles, a gnarly Fender Rhodes track, trippy lyrics - and it all comes together.

Day Tripper - aside from being a fun rock song with an iconic guitar line, this one has a special memory attached for me. In my senior year of high school, we did a production of Bye Bye Birdie, and this was my audition song for the lead role, which I also taught myself to play on guitar. Unfortunately, they said I wasn't "sleazy" enough, and I didn't get the part.

Drive My Car - a well crafted pop song with just enough elements of sophistication, and just plain fun.

Eleanor Rigby - a great example of the dark, classical feel of the music matching and amplifying the sombre tone of the lyrics. Kudos to George Martin for his major role in making that happen.

Get Back - Cool stylized vocal by Paul, cool keyboard solo by Billy Preston.

Hey Jude - another one that has a special memory for me. I was singing backgrounds with Kenny Loggins at the 1993 Earth Day concert at the Hollywood Bowl. Before Paul went out to do his show closing performance, he gathered us all backstage and said that he wanted everyone there to join him for 'Hey Jude' at the end of his set. We did, it rocked, and as the last note rang out, Paul, who I had never met before, looked across the stage straight at me, and walked over and shook my hand before thanking everyone else. It was a memory of a lifetime for me, right up there with playing with Frank Zappa for all those years.

I Saw Her Standing There - "My heart went boom when I crossed that room." I was a teenage boy when this came out, and what teenage boy doesn't know that feeling?

Magical Mystery Tour - another one with a memory, this one kind of funny. The band I had with my high school buddies used to practice in a paint store owned by the drummer's dad. We were there practicing one Sunday right when the church across the street finished their service and everyone was streaming out. Being somewhat irreverent and rebellious teenagers, we opened up the door of the paint shop and struck up a rousing rendition of 'Magical Mystery Tour' to send the congregation on their way.

Sgt. Pepper's Lonely Hearts Club Band - yet another one with lots of vivid memories, too many to detail, but most connected with that same high school band touring the northeast states in the summer of '68 with a singer from Philadelphia named Bunny Sigler. We played chitlin' circuit clubs, and started Bunny's show by ourselves with about fifteen minutes of music from the ground breaking Sgt. Pepper album that had come out the summer before, playing to an all black audience that couldn't quite figure out what we were thinking. Since I play French horn, we even included the iconic horn lines on the title track. Then Bunny would come on and we would play Knock On Wood, Soul Man, Hold On I'm Comin', Funky Broadway, etc. Somehow, it all worked, and because the audience could see that we loved and understood music that seemed to come from such disparate places, they came to love it too.

We Can Work It Out - Aside from the fact that the title is a good concept for all humans to grasp, it comes as part of the new propensity the Beatles began to show for experimentation and innovation in the *Rubber Soul* and *Revolver* albums that hinted at what was to come in Sgt. Pepper.

With A Little Help From My Friends - one of those unusual instances where, for me, the much "churchier" remake by Joe Cocker really digs into the potential of the song, and far surpasses the lightweight, throwaway approach the Beatles gave it.

Yesterday - just a great, classic, young love song that I think rings true and hits a spot in nearly everyone's heart at some point in their life. That's what music's about, crafting sound into a shape that moves the listener.

Acknowledgements

Thanks to...
My family: Julie, Chris, Emma and Lizzy (for fun and fracking); Mum, Steve, Lynn, Paul, Michelle, Trevor, 'Geoff', Simon...and the 'outlaws'. Love y'all.
My friends: John Campbell, Ian Day, Helen Tate, Mick Zeuner, Mick Ekers, Heather Webster, Jamie Bird, Dave Spooner, Ariane Mendoza, Lee Clutton, Jo & Kim Hawkins, Jerry Bloom (for your forbearance), and all those in my Zappa and Facebook communities (too numerous to mention, but I reckon you know who you are).

The contributors to 'Things We Said Today' – some are dead and some are living.
And finally: John, Paul, George & Ringo.

About the author...

Andrew Greenaway was born in Orpington, Kent, in 1958. He edits the UK's only Frank Zappa website (www.idiotbastard.com) and has compiled four Zappa-themed albums for Cordelia Records (one of which includes 'deranged' covers of 'Norwegian Wood' and 'I Am The Walrus' – seek them out).

As well as writing *Zappa The Hard Way* for Wymer in 2010, Andrew contributed to *1001 Songs You Must Hear Before You Die* (Octopus Books, 2010), *We Are The Other People - 25 Years Of Zappanale* (Synergia Verlag, 2014) and *The Greatest Albums You'll Never Hear* (Octopus Books, 2014). He also helped 'ghost' Anton Johnson's autobiography *King Of Clubs* (Grosvenor House, 2012).

Currently co-hosting a fortnightly rock show on Thurrock Community Business Radio and one of the key contributors to ZappaCast - The Frank Zappa Podcast, Andrew also made a guest appearance - along with Robert Martin and Scott Carter Thunes - on J21's album *Beyond The Holographic Veil* (Floating World Records, 2011).

Andrew has three children, two cats, and lives with his wife Julie near the Thames Delta in deepest, darkest Essex. His hobbies are films, reading, Chelsea FC, Speedway GP, smiling and, of course, music.